THE WIPERS TIMES

by Ian Hislop and Nick Newman

SAMUEL FRENCH

ISBN 978-0-573-11351-2

concordtheatricals.co.uk
concordtheatricals.com

FOR PRODUCTION ENQUIRIES

UNITED KINGDOM AND WORLD
EXCLUDING NORTH AMERICA
licensing@concordtheatricals.co.uk

020-7054-7298

NORTH AMERICA
info@concordtheatricals.com
1-866-979-0447

Each title is subject to availability from Concord Theatricals, depending upon country of performance.

THE WIPERS TIMES
By Ian Hislop and Nick Newman

First presented at The Watermill Theatre on
22nd September 2016 with the following cast:

Kevin Brewer – Henderson/Optimism Doctor/Chaplin/MC/
Doctor Supitup

Eleanor Brown – Kate Roberts/Secretary/Smith/Bobbing
Bobby/Nurse/Madame Fifi/Lady Somersby

Sam Ducane – Lt Colonel Howfield/MC/Churchill/Photographer

James Dutton – Captain Fred Roberts

George Kemp – Lieutenant Jack Pearson/Bellory Helloc

Peter Losasso – Dodd/MC/Higgins

Jake Morgan – Barnes/Optimism Patient

Dan Tetsell – Deputy Editor/Tyler/Mitford/Teach Bomas

Director – **Caroline Leslie**
Designer – **Dora Schweitzer**
Lighting Designer – **James Smith**
Sound Designer – **Steve Mayo**
Composer – **Nick Green**
Musical Director – **Paul Herbert**
Movement Director – **Emily Holt**
Dialect Coach – **Mary Howland**
Assistant Director – **Chloe France**

A Trademark Touring Ltd & Watermill Theatre Ltd Production

For the original production, archive stills and film were
used to illustrate the action. These are not essential to any
future production.

ABOUT THE AUTHORS

IAN HISLOP

Ian Hislop is a writer and broadcaster and has been editor of *Private Eye* since 1986. He has been a columnist for *The Listener* and *The Sunday Telegraph*, and TV critic for *The Spectator*. As a scriptwriter with Nick Newman, his work includes five years on *Spitting Image, Harry Enfield and Chums*, and *My Dad's The Prime Minister*, and the film *A Bunch of Amateurs*. He has written and presented many documentaries for TV and radio including: *Radio 4s The Real Patron Saints, A Brief History of Tax, Are We Being As Offensive As We Might Be, Lord Kitchener's Image, The Six Faces of Henry VIII* and *I've Never Seen Star Wars*; and presented TV's *Great Railway Journeys – East to West, Scouting for Boys, Not Forgotten, Ian Hislop Goes Off The Rails, Ian Hislop's Changing of the Bard, Age of the Do-Gooders, When Bankers Were Good, Stiff Upper Lip: An Emotional History of Britain, Ian Hislop's Olden Days* and *Victorian Benefits: Workers and Shirkers*. He has appeared frequently on *Question Time* and since 1990 has been team captain on BBC's *Have I Got News For You* which has won many awards, including the BAFTA for Best Comedy 2016.

Most recently he and Nick Newman wrote the critically acclaimed 2016 Radio 4 comedy drama *Trial By Laughter*. In 2014 their play *A Bunch of Amateurs* was premiered and had a successful run at The Watermill Theatre.

NICK NEWMAN

Nick Newman is a cartoonist and writer who attended Oxford University where he began selling cartoons to *Yachting Monthly* magazine in 1976. By 1981 he was working regularly for *Private Eye*, where he has drawn gags and written jokes ever since. In 1989 he became Pocket Cartoonist for *The Sunday Times* and his cartoons and strips have appeared in many other publications including *The Guardian, The Daily Telegraph, Punch* and *The Spectator*. The Cartoon Art Trust voted him Pocket Cartoonist of the Year (1997) and Gag Cartoonist of the Year (1998 and 2005). He won the Sports Journalists' Association's Award for Sports Cartoonist of the year in 2005, 2007, 2009 and 2012. In 2013 he edited the humour-bestseller *Private Eye: A Cartoon History*.

His writing career began at school, working on revues with Ian Hislop. It continued at Oxford and after working as a journalist on *Management Today* magazine, Newman worked with Hislop on *Spitting Image*, before writing for Maureen Lipman and co-writing several episodes of *Murder Most Horrid* for Dawn French. Radio credits include several series of Dave Podmore for

Radio 4 with Christopher Douglas and Andrew Nickolds as well as *Gush, News at Bedtime, What Went Wrong with the Olympics?* and *Greed All About It* with Ian Hislop. Television credits also include *Clive Anderson Talks Back*, the Screen One film *Gobble*, two series of *My Dad's The Prime Minister* for BBC 1 and sketches for *The Harry Enfield Show* – with the creation of one of its most memorable characters, Tim-Nice-But-Dim. In 2008, their film *A Bunch of Amateurs* starring Burt Reynolds was chosen for the Royal Film Performance. Their 2013 BBC 2 film *The Wipers Times* won the Broadcasting Press Guild award for best single drama, and was nominated for a BAFTA.

THE WIPERS TIMES – FROM PAGE TO STAGE

"No one is interested in the First World War". That's what we were told when we first pitched the idea of *The Wipers Times* to a film company nearly fifteen years ago. Now that the play is on the stage, we hope that's wrong.

The story of *The Wipers Times* has been a hundred years in the telling. What has ended up as a stage play began as a TV film but originated in the spring of 1916, when a group of soldiers of the 24th Division of the Sherwood Foresters, led by Captain Fred Roberts, discovered a printing press in the bombed-out ruins of Ypres – or as it was known by the Tommies unable to pronounce it – Wipers. Aided by their civvy-street printer sergeant, Roberts and his Lieutenant, Jack Pearson, decided to use the press to print a newspaper – but not a journal of record; instead, they produced a journal of jokes. It was, by turns, subversive, mawkish, groaningly punny – and incredibly funny. It satirised the press, poked fun at the high command and saluted fallen comrades, using spoof advertisements, agony aunt columns and cod music hall routines.

Often edited under enemy fire, The Wipers Times became an instant hit with the troops on the front line. It ran from 1916 until just after the end of the war – a remarkable twenty three issues. Twelve years after the end of the war, a compilation edition was published, which included a foreword by the former editor, Fred Roberts. After that, nothing. History had a very different view of the war from that of the editors of The Wipers Times, who celebrated the camaraderie, absurdity and tragedy of life in the trenches – often on the same page. There was no place for the Wipers Times in accounts of the Great War which focused on death, futility and incompetence – all of which The Wipers' editors experienced, but which they recounted in their unique, satirical way.

Contemporary poetry and literature too were predominantly heartbreaking accounts of loss. As books such as *All Quiet on the Western Front* and plays such as *Journey's End* captured the public imagination, The Wipers Times was quietly forgotten. There's a fleeting reference to the paper in *Oh! What A Lovely War!*, but otherwise public interest in the trench newspaper was limited to keen historians of the Great War. Roberts and Pearson died in obscurity, and neither received an obituary anywhere – let alone the London Times.

Then, fifteen years ago, Ian came across The Wipers Times while working on a documentary for Radio 4. Through the paper, you could hear the clear voice of troops on the front line coming through. Here was an account of the Great War written not with hindsight, nor from the vantage point of history, but there at the time, and under enemy fire. And unlike all other accounts we had read, the story was told with immense wit and humour. It didn't matter that some of the jokes were terrible – the important thing was that they were making jokes at all. It portrayed the quintessential British characteristic of using humour as a coping mechanism. Not making fun of the war – far from it – but finding light in what was otherwise unremitting gloom.

And so we began trying to work out what The Wipers Times story actually was – encouraged by our producer friend David Parfitt (who produced the TV film and this stage version). What emerged was a story of survival, endurance and indominability – told with a gallows humour that sounded as fresh as it did a century ago. We had never seen anything like it before.

For ten years we were rejected continually and – despite (or perhaps because of) the success of shows such as *War Horse* – we eventually abandoned all hope of ever seeing *Wipers* on the screen, and began writing it as a play. We instinctively believed it would work on stage – after all, The Wipers Times relentlessly spoofed music hall acts and was full of sketches (some of which were attributed to the *Journey's End* author RC Sheriff). A third of the way into writing the stage play, however, a call came out of the blue from the head of History at the BBC. Our ten-year-old treatment had finally arrived on his desk. The BBC was preparing its 2014 Great War anniversary programming, and realised the tone was all very similar. That of *Wipers* was decidedly different. Suddenly we were commissioned to write a ninety-minute film.

So began the challenge of bringing the words on the page to life on the screen. The jokes, we turned into sketches, while the music hall parodies became actual music hall routines – with poems becoming songs. We tried to imagine the joke-writing process – of which we have some experience, though not with bombs falling on our heads. It required some judicious editing and re-writing, to eliminate the more incomprehensible jargon, but wherever possible we tried to use the authors' own words rather than our own – so that full credit could go to Fred Roberts and Jack Pearson.

Research took us to Flanders, still a fractured landscape where farmers are regularly blown up by unexploded bombs, and to France where the river Somme glides through Amiens with a tranquility it's hard to equate with events of a century ago. On the way we discovered fascinating new pieces of information – such as Michelin preparing guides to the battlefield while war was still waging. With the expert help of the BBC's *Who Do You Think You Are* we discovered what had happened to Pearson after the war (hitherto a mystery). This put us in touch with his family – and led to the unearthing of exciting new source material – the unpublished memoirs of Roberts and Pearson, provided by their descendants.

It was with some trepidation that we read the personal accounts of our heroes – but were relieved to find their voices exactly matched our image of them gleaned from The Wipers Times. Roberts was a larger-than-life adventurer and gambler. He was immensely loyal to his friends and his memoir is full of wry humour. But infuriatingly, whilst recording his first meeting with "Long" Jack Pearson, he makes no mention whatsoever of The Wipers Times. Perhaps he felt he had said all he wanted to on the matter.

Jack Pearson's brief memoir, on the other hand, wrote: "One of my most pleasant recollections of that time is the birth of 'The Wipers Times', a publication which eventually attained a certain fame". Pearson's account is a masterclass in understatement and reinforced our impression of the importance of alcohol to the men at the front. Describing a visit to a friend who was encamped near the Menin Road – the scene of some of the most relentless shelling, and now the location of the Menin Gate Memorial at Ypres – he said, "I don't mind walking up the Menin Road if I go with Johnny Walker". On returning to Ypres in 1917 for that year's offensive, he wrote: "It was never quite the same, though it maintained its reputation of being a very warm corner". This was his description of the most hellish war zone on the Front Line.

And so, after years and years of plugging away, we found ourselves at Ballywalter Park near Belfast, which was turned into the HQ at Arras, the editorial den in Ypres and the trenches of the Somme. The whizz-bangs and gas gongs whizzed, banged and chimed. "You've come to the right place," said one of our Belfast film crew, "We're good at blowing things up!" Thankfully the resulting film resonated with the viewers – and was applauded by the critics who kindly voted us Best Single Drama in the 2014 Broadcasting Press Guild Awards. A BAFTA nomination was further acknowledgement, at last, for Fred Roberts and Jack Pearson.

But for us there was unfinished business. Having started to write *Wipers* as a play, we knew we wouldn't settle until we had seen it – and hear a contemporary audience react to the jokes and skits we loved from a hundred years ago. The piece is inherently theatrical – and the emotional drive of the story is tailor-made for the intimacy of the theatre, reflecting the closeness of the writing and creative process (even in the context of a surrounding conflagration). The demands of the stage gave us the opportunity to include more songs, more jokes and more backstory – making full use of the newly found original sources at our disposal. The result, we hope, does justice to the remarkable story of some remarkable men.

And the story has a coda. Immediately our film was broadcast a congratulatory email arrived from the editor of The Times, John Witherow. Whilst thanking him, we cheekily replied that perhaps now was the time for The Times to set the record straight and give Roberts and Pearson the recognition they deserved. Two weeks later another curt email pinged through: "Look in tomorrow's Times". And there, on a full page, were huge obituaries of our heroes. Not only was it the highlight of our joint writing careers, but it was also a fitting tribute to the literary endeavours of an incredibly brave group of men – saluting the triumph of the human spirit in the face of overwhelming adversity.

Ian Hislop and Nick Newman
2016

CHARACTER NOTES

CAPTAIN FRED ROBERTS – the charismatic, larger-than-life editor of *The Wipers Times*. A former mining engineer, he's an adventurer and gambler who's not afraid to laugh at death and poke fun at his superiors while suppressing his true horror at the conduct of the war.

LIEUTENANT JACK PEARSON – Roberts's deputy and sub-editor of *The Wipers Times*. A laconic foil to the ebullient Roberts, Pearson matches him joke for joke. He has a keen interest in anything alcohol related.

SERGEANT TYLER – a former Fleet Street printer who is Roberts's Mr Fixit, becoming publisher of *The Wipers Times*. Gruff and stern – but with a dry sense of humour and a passion for printing.

PRIVATE DODD – the youngest of Roberts's men and a new arrival to the front line, he has a lot to learn about life in the trenches. He grows up fast.

PRIVATE HENDERSON – worked on tunnelling the London Underground before the outbreak of war. His mischievous sense of humour lands him in trouble.

PRIVATE BARNES – Henderson's best mate and a former coal miner. His down-to-earth soldiering belies his sensitivity – and he proves to be a natural poet.

GENERAL MITFORD – as Roberts's commanding officer he is a father-figure, and keen supporter and defender of *The Wipers Times*.

LIEUTENANT COLONEL HOWFIELD – Roberts's immediate superior who is fiercely opposed to *The Wipers Times*, and wants it closed down. Lacking any sense of humour, he fails to understand when the joke's on him.

KATE ROBERTS – Fred Roberts's wife, a teacher, who keeps the home fires burning while supplying eggs to the Red Cross. She tries to understand the reality of Roberts's painful wartime experiences.

DEPUTY EDITOR, DAILY NEWS – over-worked and over-dramatic, he is unimpressed by wartime exploits largely because he didn't fight.

LADY SOMERSBY – fierce supporter of the Temperance Movement and very close 'friend' of Lloyd George, who wants alcohol banned from the trenches – much to the horror of those fighting in them.

MADAM FIFI – alluring, seductive hostess who runs the celebrated Fifi's Bar in Amiens, where Roberts goes on leave.

CHARACTERS WHO APPEAR IN THE WIPERS TIMES JOKE PIECES INCLUDE:

HILAIRE BELLOC – the famous author of Cautionary Rhymes was dubbed Belary Helloc by *The Wipers Times* on account of his patriotic, jingoistic and wildly optimistic armchair general's account of the war in magazines back home.

WILLIAM BEACH THOMAS – the Daily Mail's illustrious war Correspondent who always seemed to write from the thick of the action – but who the men never actually saw. Mocked as Teach Bomas by *The Wipers Times*. Later knighted.

CHARACTERS

SECRETARY

DEPUTY EDITOR

CAPTAIN FRED ROBERTS

LIEUTENANT JACK PEARSON

SERGEANT TYLER

DODD

BARNES

HENDERSON

LT COLONEL HOWFIELD

GENERAL MITFORD

BOBBING BOBBY

CHURCHILL

NURSE

MADAME FIFI

KATE ROBERTS

CHAPLAIN

WOUNDED SOLDIER

LADY SOMERSBY

PRIVATE YATES

PRIVATE SMITH (NON-SPEAKING)

WINSTON CHURCHILL

FRENCH PHOTOGRAPHER FOR THE MICHELIN GUIDES

ACT ONE

Scene One

We are in a newspaper editor's office in 1931. A typewriter is on the desk. The door opens and a female SECRETARY *shows in* FRED ROBERTS, *a forty-year-old man in a cheap suit with a neat pencil moustache.*

SECRETARY Please take a seat Mr Roberts. The deputy editor won't be long.

ROBERTS Thank you.

SECRETARY Can I get you anything?

ROBERTS How about... a very large whisky? *(She looks a bit shocked)* That was a joke. I'm just a bit nervous.

SECRETARY *(she smiles)* I can offer you some tea.

ROBERTS No, I'm trying to give it up.

SECRETARY *smiles.*

ROBERTS Do you know if he received my Curriculam Vitae?

SECRETARY Oh yes.

ROBERTS And did he read it?

Pause.

SECRETARY He's a very busy man.

ROBERTS I see.

SECRETARY And he's particularly busy this afternoon.

ROBERTS Yes, what with the political situation...the economy...

ROBERTS *looks at his watch.*

ROBERTS ...lunch.

SECRETARY *(smiles again)* This is a very important newspaper...

ROBERTS So I read...in your newspaper.

    SECRETARY *smiles again.*

SECRETARY Are you sure you don't want anything?

ROBERTS A job?

    SECRETARY *exits.*

    ROBERTS *sits nervously. He checks his watch, fumbles with his briefcase from which he produces a sheaf of papers. The* **DEPUTY FEATURES EDITOR** *enters abruptly and in a hurry – he's in his thirties and wears spectacles.*

DEPUTY EDITOR Sorry to keep you waiting. Balloon's gone up. Total chaos, deadlines brought forward – printers on the warpath – all kinds of merry hell – but that's Fleet Street for you.

ROBERTS I wouldn't know about Fleet Street. But I'm familiar with merry hell.

DEPUTY EDITOR Of course, of course. The War. Very good. I couldn't go of course. Eyesight...

ROBERTS I'm sorry. You missed quite a show...

DEPUTY EDITOR Really? It must have been hell. From what I've read.

ROBERTS We had some bad times, but – well we had some good times too...

DEPUTY EDITOR I'm sure... Now I see you have impressive references here from both Mr Gilbert Frankau and Mr RC Sherrif.

ROBERTS Yes I knew them back then. When we were all working on Tenth Avenue.

DEPUTY EDITOR Tenth Avenue? In New York?

ROBERTS No. In Flanders. It was a trench. There was Oxford Street, Piccadilly Circus, Leicester Square...

DEPUTY EDITOR *(interrupting)* Yes...

So perhaps you could tell me about yourself... Mr *(checks CV)*

ROBERTS Roberts. Fred Roberts. You do have my curriculum vitae?

DEPUTY EDITOR Yes – but I want to hear about you...in your own words.

It is clear that he has not bothered to read **ROBERTS**'s *CV and they both know it.* **ROBERTS** *recites it to him whilst* **DEPUTY EDITOR** *scans it.*

ROBERTS Formerly of the North Midlands, Nottinghamshire and Derbyshire regiment otherwise known as the Sherwood Foresters...

DEPUTY EDITOR *looks a bit bored so* **ROBERTS** *moves on.*

A mining engineer by profession – I worked in the Kimberley diamond mines in South Africa until friend Fritz kicked off the firework party.

DEPUTY EDITOR I see, so you have mining qualifications...

ROBERTS Jolly useful in a pioneer battalion charged with trench repair and maintenance...

DEPUTY EDITOR Though less useful in a newspaper office.

ROBERTS Oh I don't know – digging up all that muck...

DEPUTY EDITOR *beginning to be impatient.*

DEPUTY EDITOR Yes Mr Roberts, my problem is that what we need here at the Daily News is men with relevant experience. So tell me, do you **have** any relevant experience?

ROBERTS *hands over a copy of a yellowing A5 pamphlet. It is* The Wipers Times.

(Disdainfully) The Wipers Times?

Suddenly a big explosion on stage.

Scene Two

When the smoke clears we are in a derelict basement in Ypres. On the backdrop we see a photograph of the remains of the Cloth Hall against the Ypres skyline. We hear constant shell fire. Offstage we hear it is raining. A group of dripping MEN *enter the shelter of the bombed-out building. It is a patrol of Sherwood Foresters for salvage.* PEARSON, *a lieutenant in his 30s, leads the troupe of pioneers comprising Privates* HENDERSON, SMITH, YATES, BARNES, *and* DODD *who is new to the unit. They are soaking wet and exhausted.* PEARSON *lights a cigarette.*

PEARSON Oh to be in Flanders! Now that spring is here!

BARNES It's February, sir.

PEARSON Is it, Barnes? I find it frightfully difficult to tell.

PEARSON *turns to* MEN.

Usual drill, search the place for anything we can use – preferably of the metal or timber variety. And be sharp about it. Yates, Smith – check out the back.

YATES Sir!

YATES *and* SMITH *exit. We hear the noise of more shell fire.*

HENDERSON 4.2s sir.

PEARSON That's a relief. I thought for a minute they were 5.9s.

An even louder bang.

HENDERSON Now those are 5.9s, sir.

DODD *in background looks scared and suddenly draws his bayonet.*

DODD Boche vermin!

PEARSON What the hell are you doing Dodd?

DODD Surrender or die!

PEARSON Just put your bayonet away before someone gets hurt!

DODD But it's a rat, sir.

PEARSON I am familiar with the species Dodd. We have encountered one or two since we have been in Ypres.

DODD "Ypres", sir?

PEARSON It's what the Belgians call Wipers.

DODD Oh, right, sir. Funny lot the Belgians. It's like the Napoo rum they have over here. I never seem to get any.

PEARSON Napoo is from the French, Dodd. *Il n'y en a plus.* There is no more.

DODD Well why don't they just say that sir?

BARNES returns.

BARNES Nothing here, sir.

DODD *(cheerily)* Napoo salvage, sir.

PEARSON Very good Dodd, we'll make a sapper of you yet. Carry on, lads, there must be something.

Enter in a shower of dust the young **ROBERTS**, *the Captain in charge of the platoon, with* **SERGEANT TYLER**.

PEARSON Hot for the time of year Sir?

ROBERTS Yes... Fritz's love-tokens seem to be arriving with disturbing accuracy.

TYLER That's how we know the artillery's not our own.

ROBERTS Thank you Sergeant. Sorry I'm late Pearson – got a bit delayed. The state of the roads out there really is appallin. They're full of great round holes!

PEARSON You should complain to the council Sir.

ROBERTS Quite right. But the Ypres Corporation won't do a thing about it!

PEARSON As for the state of some of the trees on the roadside...

TYLER The Boche use them for target practice Sir.

ROBERTS Yes, they're not quite as "Poplar" as they used to be.

> **ROBERTS** *is aware how terrible his joke is.* **TYLER** *laughs.*

PEARSON Very good Sir!

ROBERTS Now have the boys found me anything?

PEARSON Slim pickings I am afraid.

> **ROBERTS** *and men continue searhing.*

HENDERSON What about this sir? Boxes of paper.

PEARSON Excellent. Exactly what we are looking for to reinforce Trench 132.

DODD Really, sir?

ROBERTS No Dodd. You'll find when you've been out here for a while that paper doesn't offer much protection against crumps and whizz-bangs.

PEARSON Unless you're a red hat in HQ with a cushy job and then the paper stops you getting anywhere near the shooting gallery at all.

ROBERTS Your cynicism could become wearying Lieutenant Pearson except fortunately I find it quite amusing.

HENDERSON There's some tarpaulin here sir.

ROBERTS That might be useful.

> *They go to inspect the salvage.* **HENDERSON** *pulls the tarpaulin off to reveal a printing press. A complicated tangle of ironmongery, wheels and levers.*

TYLER Blimey!

BARNES Now what the bloody hell is that?

TYLER That, Barnes, is an Arab.

BARNES I'm not stupid, sarnt.

> **TYLER** *caresses the machine.*

TYLER The Arab is an Anglo–American hand-fed Platen Press. Probably the finest in the world. It's a manual, pedal operated printing machine patented in 1872 by Josiah Wade, manufactured in Halifax and subsequently sold all over the world. In short, it is a work of art.

BARNES So shall we smash it up?

BARNES gets out his sledgehammer and raises it up.

TYLER *(shouts)* No!

YATES *(handing TYLER a large tray)* What about these I found Sir?

TYLER Look, it's even got the blocks and trays of type.

ROBERTS How on earth do you know all this Tyler?

TYLER I was a printer in civvy street, sir.

ROBERTS Good grief. You kept quiet about that.

TYLER It didn't seem relevant to fighting Fritz, sir.

ROBERTS No. But it might be now.

Pause. There is a gleam in his eye.

Can you make it work?

TYLER She's taken a bit of a knock… Had some unwelcome visitors…type's all over the countryside…

He removes some lumps of shrapnel and masonry.

But given a bit of time, yes sir, reckon so sir.

TYLER begins to use foot pedal and the machinery clanks to life.

You see you put the ink on the plate and the rollers come down onto the typeblock and you feed in the paper then… DON'T TOUCH IT DODD!

He smacks DODD's hand.

PEARSON *(to ROBERTS)* All very interesting but what are we going to DO with it?

ROBERTS We are going to borrow it.

PEARSON Isn't that looting sir?

ROBERTS No it's temporary requisitioning of civilian facilities for military purposes.

PEARSON Sounds like looting to me.

ROBERTS Ever done any journalism Pearson?

PEARSON Good God no.

ROBERTS Excellent! Me neither. Because what we are going to do is produce a newspaper. Aren't we, sergeant?

TYLER If you say so sir.

HENDERSON What? Like the *Daily Mail*?

ROBERTS No I was thinking of something rather more accurate.

PEARSON The Times?

ROBERTS Yes! We'll call it...The...Salient...News!

Pause, as they take this in.

TYLER Doesn't really work sir.

HENDERSON I wouldn't buy that.

ROBERTS No it's good...it's a pun you see, Salient as in bit of land that juts out, and salient as in relevant, essential, pertinent.

PEARSON Oh, I see – very clever Sir.

ROBERTS *(testily)* What would you rather call it then... The Ypres Times?

HENDERSON Is it going to be in Belgian sir?

DODD We call it Wipers Sir.

ROBERTS So...*The Wipers Times*!

Another big bang. Blackout.

We hear a song that covers the scene change. These will feature throughout the play.

MEN

TAKE A WILDERNESS OF RUIN,
SPREAD WITH MUD SOME SIX FEET DEEP;
IN THIS MUD NOW CUT SOME CHANNELS,
THEN YOU HAVE THE LINE WE KEEP.

NOW YOU GET SOME WIRE THAT'S SPIKY,
THROW IT ROUND OUTSIDE YOUR LINE
GET SOME PICKETS, DRIVE IN TIGHTLY
AND ROUND THESE YOUR WIRE ENTWINE.

GET A LOT OF HUNS AND PLANT THEM,
IN A DITCH ACROSS THE WAY;
NOW YOU HAVE A WAR IN THE MAKING,
AS WAGED HERE FROM DAY TO DAY.

Scene Three

We are in **ROBERTS**'s *den, a fortified cellar in the ramparts of the medieval walled town of Ypres. We can hear distant artillery fire. There is a piano, a sofa, a few chairs, a desk and a gramophone.* **ROBERTS** *and* **PEARSON** *are drinking whisky. A sign reads "The Hotel des Ramparts – the finest accommodation in Ypres"*

ROBERTS We've got plenty of ink and plenty of paper...in fact according to Tyler the only thing we seem to be lacking is copy.

Pause.

Oh come on, it can't be that hard.

Stares into space.

PEARSON None of us are writing men. We haven't done any journalism.

ROBERTS There's a first time for everything. It can't be that hard. I think we should aim to produce something a bit like... Punch. Except with jokes.

PEARSON But what are we actually going to write **about**?

Sound of shells getting nearer and louder.

ROBERTS Damn you Fritz. I can't hear myself think. Put on the Bing Boys would you, Jack?

PEARSON *puts a record on the gramophone. We hear* If You Were The Only Girl In The World *played at full volume to cover the sound of the shells. They have to shout above the noise.*

PEARSON So will *The Wipers Times* address the big questions of the war?

ROBERTS Certainly.

PEARSON And how will we do that?

ROBERTS I propose we do so by just writing down any old thing that comes into our heads.

Enter **TYLER** *with a page proof excitedly. He has a dummy page of typeset text, a template for the future look of the paper. The page has "Title", and "Headline" printed in different typefaces and the copy itself is gobbledygook.*

TYLER Trial page proof, sir. Looks pretty good, though I say it myself. Who do I show it to, sir? Who is the editor?

ROBERTS As senior officer I am of course the editor. But I will need a sub-editor. Any volunteers Jack? Bad grammar is something which I simply will not put up with.

PEARSON *(correcting him)* Up with which you simply will not put?

Pause as **ROBERTS** *takes this in.*

ROBERTS All right Jack – the job is yours.

He clinks his glass.

Which makes you, Tyler, our publisher!

TYLER *beams at the sound of this.*

TYLER I never fancied I'd ever be a publisher, sir! Not in a pile of rubble in the middle of Flanders, anyway.

ROBERTS Well a publisher is what you are, with responsibility for the efficient production and distribution of *The Wipers Times*. Congratulations.

TYLER Thank you, sir. The only drawback to efficient publication of *The Wipers Times* is that we are short of "y"s.

ROBERTS Just as well we are not based anywhere called "Ypres" then.

PEARSON *laughs.*

TYLER Now sir, what about some copy?

ROBERTS Dammit Tyler, haven't you heard of writer's block?

TYLER Only every day, sir, come deadline time for the newspaper.

ROBERTS Oh very well Tyler. But you're very annoying!

TYLER *(cheerily)* Very good sir!

PEARSON You know he's right Fred.

ROBERTS Et tu Pearson?

> **ROBERTS** *makes a dramatic move...for the pen.*

> Well I'll hold the pen and let's see what happens. Something's bound to turn up.

> *There is a silence.*

PEARSON Fred, you are an incorrigible optimist.

> **ROBERTS** *writes down the word "Optimism".*

ROBERTS Optimism. Now there's a dangerous thing. Particularly in a war. Jack – do you suffer from optimism?

> *The lighting changes to indicate that this is a surreal comedy sketch sequence inside* **ROBERTS** *head which will appear as an article in* The Wipers Times. *We see* **ROBERTS** *carrying on writing whilst two of the* **MEN** *(*BARNES *and* HENDERSON*) appear as* **DOCTOR** *and* **PATIENT**. **DOCTOR** *in a white coat holds a stethoscope which he puts to the head of* **PATIENT**.

DOCTOR *(to audience)* Men! Are you suffering from optimism? Many are and don't know the tell-tale signs.

PATIENT Is it serious doctor?

DOCTOR I just need you to answer a few questions. Do you wake up in the morning feeling that all is going well for the Allies?

PATIENT Yes doctor.

DOCTOR Do you sometimes think that the war will end sometime in the next twelve months?

PATIENT Absolutely doctor.

DOCTOR Do you consider our leaders are competent to conduct the war to a successful issue?

PATIENT I should say so doctor.

DOCTOR Oh dear this is the worst case of cheerfulness I've encountered.

PATIENT Oh good.

DOCTOR No it's terrible. But don't worry, I promise I can cure you of optimism within two days and effectively eradicate all traces of it from your system.

PATIENT Really doctor. How are you going to do that?

DOCTOR I'm writing something for you now which should do the trick.

PATIENT Is it a prescription, doctor?

DOCTOR No it's your orders. I'm sending you to the front line.

PATIENT Thank you, doctor!

Blackout. We come out of the sketch. The lights come back up on **ROBERTS** *and* **PEARSON** *reading a page proof of the Optimism article.*

There is a back projection of the original Optimism piece from The Wipers Times. **TYLER** *is in the background stooped over type blocks composing pages letter by letter. There are printed-out pages of typeface alphabets, fonts and characters hanging up. We hear as ever the sound of artillery shells in the background.*

PEARSON I'm not sure about this piece about optimism.

ROBERTS Are you questioning the judgement of a superior officer, Pearson?

PEARSON Er...yes.

ROBERTS Good. Though, as a superior officer, of course I shall ignore you.

PEARSON Seriously Fred, you don't think you are going a bit far?

ROBERTS How can you accuse me of going too far – when the
entire 24th Division has gone precisely ten yards in the last
six months?

TYLER And that was sideways.

PEARSON Thank you, sarn't. I'm just saying we have to be
careful.

ROBERTS OK. You are right. We must be responsible. As will be
made clear in my editorial.

PEARSON You haven't written an editorial.

ROBERTS How's your shorthand?

PEARSON Non-existent.

ROBERTS Good – take this down!

> PEARSON *grabs a pen and a notebook and starts taking
> dictation.*

> Editorial: having managed to pick up a printing press –
> slightly soiled – at a reasonable price...

> PEARSON *coughs.*

> ...we have decided to produce a paper. There is much
> we would like to say in it, but the shadow of censorship
> enveloping us causes us to refer to the...

> *(taps side of nose)* war...which we hear is taking place in
> Europe...

PEARSON Careful...

ROBERTS ...in a cautious manner. We apologise for any
shortcomings in production of our paper on account of...on
account of... *(Searches for word)*

PEARSON Editorial Inexperience?

ROBERTS Quite so. We hope to publish *The Times* weekly
despite the attentions of Messrs Hun and Co...

PEARSON ...our local rivals.

ROBERTS Excellent!

PEARSON *continues writing what has become a collaborative effort.*

We take this opportunity of stating that we accept no responsibility for the views expressed...

TYLER **We**?

ROBERTS ...and **we** dissociate ourselves from any statements in the advertisements.

PEARSON Well that bit's true. We haven't got any advertisements.

ROBERTS Oh. Why not?

PEARSON There is a slight problem with potential advertisers such as shops, theatres, restaurants, small businesses etcetera...

ROBERTS What problem?

PEARSON There aren't any. They've all been blown to buggery.

ROBERTS Is that anywhere near Poperinghe?

PEARSON *(laughing)* No it isn't. You didn't hear that did you, sergeant?

TYLER No sir. But it was most amusing.

ROBERTS You're the expert, Tyler. We can't be a proper newspaper without advertisements can we?

TYLER No sir. That's what the front page is for.

PEARSON So what do we do?

On the backdrop screen we see we see a fake advertisement from The Wipers Times. *The copy reads: "TAXIS! TAXIS! TAXIS!"*

We are in a comedy sketch. Jaunty music. One of the **MEN** *as* **TOMMY** *tries to hail a taxi.*

TOMMY Taxi? Taxi? I say taxi?

ROBERTS *(voiceover)* Are you having trouble getting home? Not any more with our fleet of handsomely appointed taxi cabs!

TOMMY But how will I recognise your taxis?

ROBERTS *(voiceover)* Easy! They have a Red Cross painted on each side!

We see on the screen archive footage of World War One ambulance. We then see another fake advertisement, done as a sketch in which we see a bonneted **SWEETHEART** *(one of the* **MEN** *in drag).*

PEARSON *(voice over)* Is your friend a soldier?

SWEETHEART *nods coyly.*

(voiceover) Do you know what he wants?

SWEETHEART *coyly shakes head.*

(voiceover) No? We do. Send him one of our latest improved combination umbrella and wirecutter.

Another of the **MEN** *as* **INVENTOR** *in brown coat walks on and presents device to girl. It is a ridiculous prop of cutters with an umbrella on top.*

(voiceover) No more nasty colds caught when cutting the wire! He'll be absolutely delighted with the combination umbrella and wirecutter. Just 15 francs.

SWEETHEART *hands over money to* **INVENTOR.**

(voiceover) Quite right, miss. Now you can rest assured your soldier friend will stay fit and healthy out in no man's land!

We then see another of the **MEN** *as* **SOLDIER** *using the wirecutters as* **INVENTOR** *pours a watering can over him in demonstration. He gives a cheery thumbs up.*

We go straight into another advertisement. One of the **MEN** *dressed as* **SUBALTERN** *is standing in a trench.*

ROBERTS *(voiceover)* Calling all harassed subalterns!

SUBALTERN *(adopting posh officer voice)* Who me?

ROBERTS *(voiceover)* Yes you! Is your life miserable? Do you hate your company commander?

SUBALTERN *looks around shiftily to see if anyone is looking.*

(voiceover) Of course you do. Then why not buy him one of our new patent "Tip me up" duck boards?

SUBALTERN But how does the 'Tip Me up' Duck Board work?

ROBERTS *(voiceover)* You just get your company commander on the end...

On the backdrop screen, we see in black and white silent-movie style, one of the MEN *as a* SENIOR OFFICER *walking towards a see-saw-type plank.*

(voiceover) ...and the duck board does the rest.

SENIOR OFFICER *stands on one end of the duck board,* SUBALTERN *jumps on the other end.* SENIOR OFFICER *flies off camera with silly swannee-whistle sound effect.*

(voiceover) Every time a blighty! That's our promise. Remember: "If once he steps on to the end, twill take a month his face to mend".

SUBALTERN SMITH *gives cheeky wink and a thumbs up.*

SUBALTERN Thank you, "Tip Me Up" duck board!

Blackout.

Lights up on ROBERTS *in the den; admiring the finished blocks of type for the "Tip Me Up" duck board. We hear pouring rain outside.*

ROBERTS Excellent work, sergeant. And in case you're wondering the "Tip Me Up" duck board doesn't work for Non Commissioned Officers.

TYLER Of course not, Sir

ROBERTS So when can we roll the presses?

TYLER Just as soon as we can get these blocks onto the printer.

PEARSON Which is situated in agreeable bombed-out premises just a short walk away...

TYLER More of a run at the moment, sir...unless it eases off a bit...

ROBERTS Surely you're not bothered by a spot of rain?

We hear the sound of an explosion.

TYLER More the shelling, sir. Fritz is getting a bit too near to the print room to be pleasant.

ROBERTS Well as soon as Herman knocks off for an evening sausage let's leg it down there and print the blighter.

TYLER Back in Fleet Street, sir, the editorial staff are not encouraged to enter the print room.

ROBERTS Why ever not?

TYLER They tend to want to change things at the last minute.

PEARSON I think the sergeant means that we as officers would be a bit of a nuisance in the smooth running of the operation.

ROBERTS So a bit like the war.

TYLER I didn't say that, sir.

ROBERTS Carry on.

Blackout. We hear a song that covers the scene change.

MEN

    LITTLE STACKS OF SANDBAGS,
    LITTLE LUMPS OF CLAY,
    MAKE OUR BLOOMING TRENCHES,
    IN WHICH WE WORK AND PLAY.
    MERRY LITTLE WHIZZ-BANG,
    JOLLY LITTLE CRUMP,
    MADE OUR TRENCH A PICTURE,
    WIGGLE WOGGLE WUMP.

Scene Four

Empty print room. We can hear shells going off and flashes of explosions offstage.

Through the door bursts TYLER *and the* MEN, *having clearly run the gauntlet through the streets of Ypres. They are carrying the printers blocks we saw in the den.* DODD *is blown inwards on entry and falls to the floor.*

Cut to:

TYLER Everything all right?

DODD I'm fine, sarn't.

TYLER Not you – the print blocks. Come on you lot. Look lively.

They remove the tarpaulin on the printer and assume their places around it. They know their roles and TYLER *begins to pedal the machine which begins clanking to life. The roller comes down on a plate covered in ink and then onto the type block, which is then pressed onto paper.* TYLER *removes the sheet of paper and puts in another one. The process is repeated. The* MEN *help with the process of folding, collating and stacking printed sheets.*

Don't get your hand caught in the plate, Barnes, or you'll come a cropper – a phrase incidentally derived from the printing presses of HS Cropper...

BARNES That's very interesting, sarnt.

It isn't. Barnes is taking the mickey.

TYLER ...as is the phrase 'mind your Ps and Qs, owing to the common mistaking of the P for the Q in the tray of type...

BARNES That's even more interesting, sarn't.

Barnes is smirking.

TYLER Whereas the expression "to get the wrong end of the stick" comes from the misuse of the compositing stick.

HENDERSON And means "thinking you're being interesting when really you're being..."

TYLER Yes, Henderson?

HENDERSON Very very interesting indeed, sarnt.

TYLER Correct.

> **TYLER** *is tolerant about being ribbed by the two* **MEN**.

> *The printed issue comes out of printer.* **DODD** *hands it to* **TYLER** *who holds it up proudly.*

DODD Here it is, sarn't.

TYLER The end result, though I say it myself, is a thing of beauty.

> *Beat.*

Unlike any of you.

> *Enter* **ROBERTS** *and* **PEARSON** *with knapsack. The* **MEN** *all stand to attention.*

PEARSON At ease.

ROBERTS Don't worry, sarn't, I'm not going to change a word – but I simply couldn't wait to see the fruit of our labours.

PEARSON No. Didn't want to miss our first press day! Hold the front page! Read all about it and so on!

> **TYLER** *is amused by the attempts at jargon and hands the two* **MEN** *copies of the paper.*

TYLER What do you think, sir?

ROBERTS I think...this calls for champagne!

> **ROBERTS** *fishes out a bottle from bag.*

PEARSON Where on earth did you get that?

ROBERTS I had a bit of luck at cards with some of the brass hats billeted at the chateau. Frightfully good cellar as it turned out...

MEN *laugh.* **ROBERTS** *is performing a launching ceremony.*

Thought it might come in handy to launch our new venture. In the absence of Her Majesty Queen Mary, you will have to make do with me!

Pause.

God bless this printer, and all the jokes who fail in her!

He looks as if he is going to break it on the side of the printer like a ship.

TYLER Be careful with the printer, sir!

PEARSON Be careful with the champagne more like! You can't waste that. There's a war going on.

ROBERTS Is there? I had no idea. Well in that case we'd better make sure that the Germans don't get hold of it.

He pops the cork and pours it into various tin mugs which are laid out on a tray and hands them out to the assembled **MEN, DODD, BARNES** *and* **HENDERSON** *who are thrilled to be drinking it.*

To *The Wipers Times*!

ALL *The Wipers Times*!

We hear the song to cover the scene change.

MEN

THROUGH TRIALS AND TRIBULATIONS,
AND DISASTERS EVERY DAY,
NO CAUSE FOR CELEBRATIONS,
THE CAPTAIN'S GOING GREY.

LIFE IS FULL OF DISAPPOINTMENTS,
DAYS ARE NEVER FREE FROM CARE,
FOR IN SPITE OF USING OINTMENTS,
THE COLONEL'S LOSING ALL HIS HAIR.

Scene Five

Divisional HQ in Arras. The office of GENERAL
MITFORD. MITFORD *is sitting at his desk reading a
copy of* The Wipers Times, *when a young gung-ho staff
officer* LIEUTENANT COLONEL HOWFIELD *enters angrily.*
GENERAL MITFORD *is the older, more tolerant officer – he
puts away his magazine.*

HOWFIELD Have you seen this poppycock, sir?

Howfield slams The Wipers Times *down on the desk.*

MITFORD Yes I think I have. I hear it's becoming very popular.

HOWFIELD It's downright insubordination.

MITFORD That may be why the men seem to like it.

HOWFIELD The men also like the ladies of the Poperinghe
Fancies but neither are exactly conducive to winning the
war.

MITFORD Really? Have you seen the ladies of the Poperinghe
Fancies?

HOWFIELD Of course not!

MITFORD Well I'd say they are doing their bit...jolly buxom
girls. They can't sing and they can't dance but no-one seems
to care particularly. I believe the chaps call them Glycerine
and Vaseline, I have no idea why...

HOWFIELD We're getting off the point here, sir which is surely
that some of the material in this publication is not merely
unsuitable but is downright treasonable.

MITFORD Like what in particular?

HOWFIELD Like this...

HOWFIELD passes MITFORD *the magazine.*

MITFORD Ah yes...the answers to correspondents...

HOWFIELD Whoever wrote this should be court martialled.

MITFORD *studies page.*

MITFORD The item advising young officers not to wear turned up slacks and shoes when going over the top?

HOWFIELD What!

MITFORD Perfectly sound advice. A chap wearing turned up slacks on the battlefield not only looks bloody silly but advertises the fact that he is an officer to any half-awake sniper.

HOWFIELD *snatches the paper back and reads it out.*

HOWFIELD That's not the offending article. I am referring to this reply to a supposed query from a junior officer.

(He reads out) "Dear Subaltern – no, the death penalty is **not** enforced in the case of murdering a senior officer as you will always be able to claim extenuating circumstances".

MITFORD *cannot disguise his amusement.*

MITFORD It's a joke.

HOWFIELD It's an incitement to mutiny. I'll have him shot.

MITFORD NOT if he shoots you first.

Pause.

That is also a joke.

HOWFIELD The war is not funny, sir.

MITFORD I think the authors are aware of that. I've a feeling that may be the point. And it's not **all** cocking a snook at the General Staff.

MITFORD *flicks through magazine.*

Although admittedly quite a lot of it is. No, some of it is deadly serious. Words from the heart.

HOWFIELD Such as?

MITFORD *takes magazine back and quotes aloud.*

MITFORD "People we take our hats off to: the French of Verdun... the British Navy at Jutland... The Canadians at Ypres". Saluting our fallen comrades is hardly sedition is it?

HOWFIELD They also take their hats off to the officer in charge of the costume department of the Poperinghe Fancies.

MITFORD *laughs.*

You see – they are just a gang of backchat comedians deliberately undermining morale with this impertinent, unpatriotic rag. Can you think of anything more likely to produce discontent amongst the men?

MITFORD Yes. Banning it.

Large explosion signals scene change. When smoke clears, we are in a trench.

Scene Six

A trench. The pioneers are working in foul conditions shoring up a collapsed trench with corrugated iron and timber. Shells explode and flares light up no man's land.

ROBERTS How are we doing on timber?

PEARSON The sergeant's taken a detail to scrounge some more from the communications line.

BARNES appears with YATES carrying timber.

Good work Barnes, Yates.

ROBERTS Where's Henderson?

Enter HENDERSON doing up trousers.

HENDERSON Sorry, sir, call of nature. Number two ammo dump.

BARNES Spare us the detail Hendo.

HENDERSON Tell you what, though – that *The Wipers Times* does what it says on the cover. Very handy...

HENDERSON stuffs remains of issue of The Wipers Times *back in his pocket.*

ROBERTS As is this shovel...

ROBERTS hands HENDERSON a shovel. The men get to work.

Now take Dodd and start shoring up the parapets.

BARNES *(groans)* We didn't sign up for babysitting, sir.

PEARSON Just get on with it, Barnes.

HENDERSON Are we being punished, sir?

ROBERTS No, Dodd is. Having to work with you two.

They laugh.

BARNES Fair enough.

They get to work.

PEARSON So what's the plan, sir?

ROBERTS What we need to do, Jack, is...up the cover price, get in some new writers and cut down on the poetry.

PEARSON You don't think you might be getting rather obsessed with the paper...

ROBERTS Obsessed? I'm not obsessed! Don't be ridiculous, Jack. I'm a model commanding officer executing my duties in exemplary fashion.

Beat.

So what do YOU think of the poetry?

PEARSON I think poetry is essential in the modern battlefield, sir. A bit like mud.

ROBERTS If only it were just mud.

ROBERTS *and* **PEARSON** *look at what they are up to their knees in which we imagine contains effluent, body parts of horses and humans.*

PEARSON Probably better not to dwell on the...unmentionables. Best left unsaid.

ROBERTS That's why I would rather think about the paper. It's important to me because...it is not important.

PEARSON Oh dear. You're getting aphoristic.

ROBERTS Am I? My apologies.

ROBERTS *consults mao of trench.*

So what are our tactics?

PEARSON *thinks.*

PEARSON I suggest we crack out another couple of issues, and if it keeps going this well, try and sell the paper back home.

ROBERTS You don't think you might be getting rather... what's the word?... Obsessed?

PEARSON *laughs.* **ROBERTS** *sees* **DODD** *out of the corner of his eye.* **DODD** *is striking a match with a cigarette in his mouth.*

What the hell do you think you are doing, Dodd?

DODD *(smiling cheerily and using the words of "Pack Up Your Troubles")* I'm striking a Lucifer to light my fag, Sir..

ROBERTS Well don't unless you want a sniper to take your bloody head off.

DODD *quickly extinguishes cigarette.*

DODD Sorry sir.

He throws the cigarette down.

TYLER You've got a lot to learn son...like don't waste a good Woodbine...

TYLER *picks up discarded fag and puts it behind his own ear.* **HENDERSON** *and* **BARNES** *laugh. In the background we can hear German troops singing. It is melodic and appears uplifting.*

ROBERTS Listen lads. Fritz is in fine voice.

DODD What are they singing, sir? Sounds like a hymn, sir.

ROBERTS It is. It is called the Hymn of Hate.

PEARSON *(translating)* It goes something like this.

He talks over the singing.

YOU WE WILL HATE WITH A LASTING HATE,
WE WILL NEVER FOREGO OUR HATE,
HATE BY WATER AND HATE BY LAND,
HATE OF THE HEAD AND HATE OF THE HAND.

ROBERTS *joins in. The two of them sing along with the Germans in translation.*

ROBERTS AND PEARSON
HATE OF THE HAMMER AND HATE OF THE CROWN,
HATE OF SEVENTY MILLIONS CHOKING DOWN.
WE LOVE AS ONE, WE HATE AS ONE,

WE HAVE ONE FOE AND ONE ALONE – ENGLAND!

DODD That's not very nice is it, sir.

ROBERTS Spot on, Dodd.

DODD We don't have any songs like that do we, sir?

ROBERTS No we don't. And if we did they would certainly be a lot funnier.

DODD I think your Wipers Times should put that right, sir.

PEARSON Good idea, Dodd!

ROBERTS Yes – since Dodd appears to have joined the editorial conference, I suggest we take his excellent suggestion on board and include something suitably melodious in the next issue.

PEARSON What do you have in mind?

DODD We all love the music hall, sir.

Blackout as music strikes up.

Scene Seven

*When the lights come back on we are in a fantasy music
hall where one of our* MEN *is dressed as the compere of
an old-time music hall like the* MC *character in "The
Good Old Days". There is a screen in the background
with the spoof musical advertisement for the Cloth Hall
from* The Wipers Times.

MC Ladies and Gentlemen welcome to the Cloth Hall at Ypres,
the best ventilated hall in the town!

*On the screen we see famous black and white photo of
destroyed Cloth Hall at Ypres.*

The only venue where you can see all the stars.

YATES *holds up cue cards for the audience with appropriate
responses written on them. We hear a music-hall audience
cheering.*

Tonight for your delectation we proudly present
positively the greatest collection of entertainers ever
collected in one place in one time. Yes, it is Mr Thomas
Atkins in his stupendous new revue "The Bing Bangs
Are Here"!

*On the screen we see footage of Tommies under artillery
fire.*

AUDIENCE *(offstage)* Ooh!

MC With music by Mr R Tillery

*As he says this on the screen we see footage of British
gun recoiling as it fires.*

AUDIENCE Aahh!

MC And a special accompaniment by Mrs Mini Werfer who
always meets with a thunderous reception.

AUDIENCE Boo!!

*On the screen we see large a German trench mortar
exploding.*

MC And introducing the world's favourite comedian Kaiser Bill...

On the screen we see the Kaiser inspecting the troops. The audience laugh.

...and his Little Willie...

AUDIENCE *(tickled by double entendre)* Wahay!

MC *bangs a gavel.*

MC That's the Crown Prince I'm talking about, thank you.

On the screen we see a photograph of the Crown Prince.

But first I promised you a song and a song you shall have – a pleasing patriotic performance from our very own Sapper Brothers...

SAPPER BROTHERS (BARNES *and* **HENDERSON)** *perform a duet.*

HENDERSON
I HEARD THE BUGLES CALLING
COME AND JOIN THE NOBLE FIGHT
YOU KNOW YOUR COUNTRY NEEDS YOU
AND YOU KNOW THE CAUSE IS RIGHT.

BARNES
I HEARD THE BUGLES CALLING
THERE WAS DUTY TO BE DONE
SAY FAREWELL TO YOUR SWEETHEART
AND HELLO TO THE HUN.

BARNES AND HENDERSON
I HEARD THE BUGLES CALLING
AND JOIN UP I FELT I MUST
NOW I WISH I HAD LEFT THEM BUGLES
GO ON BLOWING TILL THEY BUST!

Massive cheers from audience.

MC Yes – this show is going to run and run. And run. And run. And run. And run. And... RUN!!!

We hear machine gun fire and the MEN run off stage.

Blackout.

To cover scene change we hear a female voice singing. It is Kate Roberts, Fred's wife.

DO YOU REMEMBER DEAREST,
THAT DAY UPON HAMPSTEAD HEATH,
WITH THE BLUE, BLUE SKY ABOVE US
AND THE GREEN GREEN GRASS BENEATH?
OUR TWO HEARST WERE JOINED AS ONE, DEAR
AS WE WALKED THROUGH THE LEAFY GLADE
AND WISHED THAT OUR TIME WASN'T DONE, DEAR
AS THE LIGHT BEGAN SLOWLY TO FADE

WHEN OUR PRECIOUS HOURS HAD ENDED,
TOGETHER WE WALKED AWAY,
AS THE SHADOWS OF NIGHT DESCENDED
AT THE CLOSE OF OUR LOVE TOGETHER,
AH! SWEET WAS THE OLD REFRAIN:
YOU SAID YOU'D BE WITH ME FOREVER,
THEN YOU RAN TO CATCH THE LAST TRAIN.

Scene Eight

ROBERTS and PEARSON are looking at proofs of the music hall page. They are relaxed, drinking whisky and smoking. Melancholy music on gramophone. DODD enters.

DODD Letters for you, sir.

He gives one to ROBERTS and one to PEARSON. ROBERTS opens his.

ROBERTS Thank you Dodd. How are you getting on with those rats?

DODD They eat everything, sir. My cake from home, my bully beef, they even ate my sardines, sir.

PEARSON How did they get into the tin?

DODD That's the odd thing, sir. It looked like they used the key.

PEARSON Um... I smell a rat, eh, sir.

ROBERTS I think, Dodd, maybe you need to have a word with a rodent of a different variety – you could start with Henderson.

DODD Yes, sir.

PEARSON Thank you, Dodd.

DODD exits puzzled. The two officers open their letters and the mood turns thoughtful.

ROBERTS Ah – news from the home front. Has my wife been raising money for noble causes such as providing warm woollens for war worn walloons?

PEARSON Or has my mother been selling flags for blue body belts for Bucolic Belgians?

ROBERTS Touché!

They open their letters and read in silence.

We see KATE ROBERTS in spotlight.

KATE My dearest Fred, life here continues much the same and my letters must seem very boring to you. Still, I must tell you about the chickens. They are now laying eggs for wounded soldiers attended by the Red Cross – and so are doing their bit for the war effort. I have made little red crosses to hang around the chickens' necks so that people know that they are proper war workers! I also draw a red cross on the eggs to make it clear that our chicks are supporting our boys.

ROBERTS *chuckles.*

I'm not complaining, because it's nothing compared with what you must be enduring, but we are short of most things.

Coal, meat, butter, cheese – but most of all we are short of laughter. And that is because you, darling Fred, are not here.

Light fades on KATE.

ROBERTS Always a bit of a mixed blessing isn't it – the letter from home?

PEARSON A reminder of a land without the gas gong, whizz-bangs and Minenwerfers.

ROBERTS Good heavens – my wife has sent me a clipping from the Tatler. We've been mentioned in despatches!

PEARSON *(excited)* Really? Fame at last! What does it say?

ROBERTS *(reads out from little piece of paper)* "We hear news from the front of an amusing periodical designed to entertain the troops. It is entitled *The Wipers Times* after the town of Ypres where its enterprising creators are currently quartered. So we salute the anonymous wits of the 6th Division..."

PEARSON What?! We're the **24th** Division you nincompoops!

ROBERTS Oh dear. It appears that we are not to be famous after all.

PEARSON Damned journalists. Can't they get anything right?

ROBERTS Is that a rhetorical question?

TYLER *enters with field phone.*

TYLER It's Lieutenant Colonel Howfield's ADC, sir.

ROBERTS Oh no. Little Bobbing Bobbie?

PEARSON The one who has red staff flashes on his jim-jams?

> **ROBERTS** *takes the phone.*

ROBERTS Ah captain. How can I help you? Of course yes. No time like the present. Looking forward to it, sir.

> *Puts phone down.*

> Thank you, sergeant. Lieutenant Colonel Hector Alexander Horatio Howfield has granted us the privilege of a full inspection.

PEARSON God, when?

ROBERTS Now!

PEARSON Where's that "Tip me up" duck board when you need it?

ROBERTS No need for alarm. Sergeant, initiate Operation Panic!

> *They hit panic stations and both jump up and start clearing away proofs, trays of type and paraphernalia of printing.*

TYLER Barnes, Dodd, get in here and help clear the decks.

> *The two* **MEN** *arrive in the den and start clearing up.*

BARNES Are we under attack, sir?

ROBERTS Quite the reverse. We've got an inspection by the Divisional Staff. Which means that for as long as they are here there won't be **any** action at all.

> *They carry on removing and hiding the evidence of the paper.*

PEARSON And even our own artillery wouldn't dare open fire on us whilst there is a brass hat here.

All evidence of the newspaper has been removed or hidden. SMITH *enters.* PEARSON *and* ROBERTS *smarten up and straighten their caps.*

As the old adage has it... Warfare. Long periods of boredom punctuated by sheer terror.

As soon as the den is cleared, HOWFIELD *enters. The* MEN *stand to attention. We see very worried looking* PEARSON, *insouciant* ROBERTS *and the* MEN *lined up being inspected by* LIEUTENANT COLONEL HOWFIELD *accompanied by his sycophantic ADC,* CAPTAIN BOBBY, *who sports a very silly Charlie Chaplin-style moustache.*

ROBERTS Sir!

HOWFIELD At ease, Roberts. Hope I am not interrupting anything?

ROBERTS No, sir.

HOWFIELD Well I **should** be shouldn't I? Boche obviously not keeping you occupied. And vice versa. You have got time on your hands, Roberts. And time is the soldier's greatest enemy. Isn't it, Bobby?

BOBBY Yes, sir.

ROBERTS *(to* BOBBY*)* Apart from the gas and the flamethrowers...

HOWFIELD So are your boys fit, Roberts?

ROBERTS As a fiddle, sir.

HOWFIELD Because the men have got to be fit for the big push. Haven't they, Bobby?

BOBBY Very fit, sir.

HOWFIELD And what about **you**, Roberts? Keeping busy?

ROBERTS As a bee, sir.

HOWFIELD So no distractions? Finding enough to do?

ROBERTS Yes, sir doing our best to make a little cover for the lads who are holding on to the remnants of Belgium in the teeth of every disadvantage, discomfort and peril, sir.

HOWFIELD *(meaningfully staring* **ROBERTS** *in the eye)* So not too much **paperwork** then?

ROBERTS Not at all, sir.

HOWFIELD That's good to hear. Isn't it, Bobby?

BOBBY Yes, sir.

HOWFIELD Because the problem with the whole damned line is inaction. We are getting bogged down in a mire of defensive passivity. There's no forward movement – no sorties, no raiding parties, no mining activity...

ROBERTS That's right sir, its almost as if we were...entrenched.

> **HOWFIELD** *does not get joke although* **PEARSON** *is trying to keep a straight face.*

HOWFIELD *(doesn't get the joke)* Quite so.

And the question you have to ask yourself, and you particularly as commander Roberts, is, are you being offensive enough?

ROBERTS I am not sure, sir. Are we being offensive enough Pearson?

PEARSON No, sir. We're not being nearly as offensive as we could be.

HOWFIELD So you think you could be MORE offensive?

PEARSON Oh yes Sir – I think we could be MUCH more offensive.

> **ROBERTS** *and* **PEARSON** *are hugely enjoying the joke, biting their lips to repress laughter.*

HOWFIELD Quite right, Pearson. So from now you are going to be a lot, lot more offensive!

ROBERTS You hear that men? From now on we are all going to be as offensive as possible.

HOWFIELD That's very good, Roberts. Isn't it, Bobby?

BOBBY I'm not altogether sure, Sir.

There is a pause.

HOWFIELD Well that all seems to be in order. Carry on.

HOWFIELD *and* **BOBBY** *exit. Everyone bursts out laughing.*

ROBERTS Thank you, gentlemen. You are dismissed.

TYLER *and the* **MEN** *file out. We artillery fire beginning – BIG noise..*

PEARSON That is the sound of top brass leaving the theatre of war.

ROBERTS Enough of your flippancy, Jack. You heard the lieutenant colonel. We must attack something.

PEARSON How about...stupid moustaches?

ROBERTS Good idea. Far too many of them around. I blame Charlie Chaplin.

There is a big explosion overhead. Lights flicker.

I say, that was a bit friendly. Put on the gramophone would you?

PEARSON *puts on the gramophone which belts out dance music. Another explosion showers them in dust.* **PEARSON** *protects the whisky.*

No, it's not enough. I will **have** to play the piano.

He doesn't have a piano. Instead he plays a song he has made up on his typewriter.

THERE ARE VARIOUS TYPES OF COURAGE
THERE ARE MANY KINDS OF FEAR
THERE ARE MANY BRANDS OF WHISKY
THERE ARE MANY MAKES OF BEER
THERE IS ALSO RUM WHICH SOMETIMES
IN OUR NEED CAN HELP US MUCH
BUT TIS WHISKY WHISKY WHISKY HANDS
THE COURAGE WHICH IS DUTCH.

He takes a huge slug of whisky and hands flask to **PEARSON**. *He begins to sing the song over again.*

Second verse, same as the first!

ROBERTS AND **PEARSON**
THERE ARE VARIOUS TYPES OF COURAGE
THERE ARE MANY KINDS OF FEAR
THERE ARE MANY BRANDS OF WHISKY
THERE ARE MANY MAKES OF BEER
THERE IS ALSO RUM WHICH SOMETIMES IN OUR NEED CAN HELP
    US MUCH
BUT TIS WHISKY WHISKY WHISKY HANDS THE COURAGE WHICH IS
    DUTCH...

Enter **TYLER** *in the midst of this, shouting above the cacophony and carrying a mangled piece of ironmongery, part of the press.*

TYLER Bad news, sir! We've had a direct hit!

ROBERTS Where, sergeant?

TYLER Print room, sir.

Shows the twisted ironmongery.

Bloody Boche. Excuse my French, sir.

ROBERTS French excused, sergeant. How bad is it?

TYLER Blown...to Poperinghe

PEARSON Can nothing be done?

TYLER I'm afraid it's finished, sir.

PEARSON It's the end of *The Wipers Times*.

PEARSON *consolingly pats* **ROBERTS** *on the back.*

It was fun whilst it lasted, Fred.

ROBERTS I've tried throughout this war to maintain my sense of humour but now I am really...unamused.

Scene Nine

A trench. The MEN *are using the metal from the printer to shore up a trench. There is shelling going on and flares overhead.*

DODD Do you ever get used to the noise, Barnsey?

BARNES It's not so bad.

DODD Are you joking?

HENDERSON What did you do before you joined up?

DODD I worked on a farm.

BARNES I worked down the mines. This is a picnic.

HENDERSON And I was a machine worker digging tunnels for the Underground.

BARNES So you won't hear us complaining about the noise.

DODD Because it's so bloody noisy.

HENDERSON Nice one, Doddy.

PEARSON arrives lugging another bit of the press.

PEARSON Good work lads. At least we are putting the old girl to some use.

BARNES Yes sir.

PEARSON A distinguished end to her literary career...as a part of a transverse wall for C4 trench number six post.

HENDERSON Yes sir.

The MEN *appear to be amused.*

PEARSON This is a solemn occasion. What are you men so amused about?

HENDERSON It's just that Captain Roberts is on grand form tonight, Sir.

PEARSON What do you mean?

BARNES The orders he gave us were not strictly according to the drill manual.

PEARSON Really?

DODD Yes sir. He said, "fall in you blank blank blank blanks, we're going up the blanking line and if we see any blanking Boche we are going to shove their blanking bombs up their blankin...shirts".

PEARSON Did he **actually** say..."shirts", Dodd?

DODD No, sir.

HENDERSON He didn't say blanking either.

PEARSON So what did he say?

There is a pause of embarrassment.

BARNES Mucking, sir. Mucking Boche with his mucking bombs, sir.

They all snigger.

PEARSON You'll have to excuse Captain Roberts. I am afraid he has taken the loss of the printer somewhat badly.

Enter **ROBERTS** *with last recognisable piece of the printer, a mangled wheel.*

ROBERTS This is the last of her, Jack.

PEARSON Perhaps we should get the padre to say a few words.

ROBERTS Nice try, Jack...

He manages a half-smile.

VOICE OFF Mind your backs. Raiding party coming through!

A **BRITISH OFFICER** *wearing a French helmet enters followed by two* **SOLDIERS** *in balaclavas.* **PEARSON** *and* **ROBERTS** *salute the* **OFFICER***.*

ROBERTS I assumed it wasn't a delegation from the General Staff.

OFFICER *(laughs)* You wouldn't see them this end of the muddy stick. You must be Roberts.

ROBERTS Sir.

OFFICER I hear you are a bit of a thorn in the red hats' backsides.

Pause.

Good man.

The raiding party moves on.

ROBERTS Good luck, colonel.

PEARSON Who was that, Fred?

ROBERTS Commanding officer of the Royal Scots Fusiliers.

PEARSON So why was he wearing a French tin hat?

ROBERTS Bit of a personality. Somewhat eccentric. Always suggesting that the top brass come to the front and get a taste of the action.

PEARSON He won't last long. What's his name?

ROBERTS Churchill.

*   **TYLER** *enters trench carrying a large, very heavy canvas bag over his houlder, while keeping his head down.*

TYLER Watch out, Dodd!

DODD It's like bloomin' Piccadilly Circus here!

PEARSON Hence the name I would guess.

Holds up hand painted sign saying "Piccadilly Circus".

ROBERTS Where have you been, Sergeant?

TYLER Had to check out a rumour, sir.

ROBERTS Don't tell me. The Kaiser has been arrested by Field Marshall Hindenberg and shot as a spy.

TYLER Not exactly, sir. A friend of a friend of a friend told me that he just happened to know the whereabouts of a lovely little hand-jigger.

PEARSON Speak English, sergeant.

TYLER A hand-jigger is a portable printing press, sir, and my friend of a friend...

PEARSON Yes, yes, sergeant...

TYLER Anyway, he said that not only was it a working printer but there was also a lot more type...

ROBERTS is suddenly taking a big interest.

ROBERTS That's priceless, sergeant.

TYLER Only one drawback, sir. Its location.

PEARSON Namely?

TYLER Hellfire Corner.

PEARSON Oh dear. That's **the** Hellfire Corner, the most dangerous spot on the salient.

TYLER Hottest place in the world, sir.

ROBERTS Where life expectancy is about what...sixty seconds?

TYLER If that, sir...

ROBERTS It would be an act of some folly to risk lives rescuing a printing press – so no sensible commanding officer could possibly sanction it. Is that clear?

TYLER I thought you would say that, sir, which is why I already went and got it.

He reveals the portable hand-jigger.

ROBERTS You know what this means, sergeant?

TYLER Court martial, sir?

ROBERTS It means *The Wipers Times* is back in business!

Men cheer.

Blackout.

Scene Ten

On the screen we see the spoof advertisement for the music hall from The Wipers Times *for the Neuve Eglise Hippodrome and the revue "Over the Top". We are again in the fantasy world of* **ROBERTS***'s imagination.*

MC Ladies and gentlemen, welcome to the latest venue on our grand tour of Flanders – the Neuve Eglise Hippodrome, where our doors are always open.

Audience cheers. Shot on the screen of bombed-out church.

Tonight we are honoured to present a show to die for – the grand new revue "Over the Top", positively the greatest spectacular performance ever staged.

Starring Bouncing Bertha who is only seventeen-inches high but is guaranteed to bring the house down.

As he says this, on the screen we see a seventeen-inch shell being fed into a large German canon, which then fires on the building, which collapses.

AUDIENCE Oooh!

MC Not forgetting the incomparable Hind and Berg, sword swallowers and nail-eaters.

On the screen we see footage of German troops in trenches.

AUDIENCE Booo!

MC But topping the bill it's musical merriment from our very own sapper songbirds, Trench and Foot, with their delightful ditty "Minor Worries".

Flannagan and Allen-style music hall song performed by **TRENCH AND FOOT** (**HENDERSON** *and* **BARNES***) using their rifles as canes.*

TRENCH AND FOOT
   IF THE HUN LETS OFF SOME GAS – NEVER MIND
   IF THE HUN ATTACKS IN MASS – NEVER MIND

IF YOUR DUG-OUT'S BLOWN TO BITS
OR THE CO'S THROWING FITS
OR A CRUMP YOUR RUM JAR HITS, NEVER MIND.

Audience cheer.

IF YOUR TRENCH IS MUD KNEE-HIGH NEVER MIND,
YOU CAN'T FIND A SPOT THAT'S HIGH NEVER MIND,
IF A SNIPER HAS YOU SET,
THROUGH DENTS IN YOUR PARAPET
AND YOUR TROUBLES FIERCER GET NEVER MIND.

Audience cheer and wolf-whistle.

IF MACHINE GUNS JOIN THE MUDDLE NEVER MIND,
THOUGH YOU'RE LYING IN A PUDDLE NEVER MIND,
IF A DUCK BOARD BARKS YOUR SHIN
AND THE BARBED WIRE RIPS YOUR SKIN
'TIS REWARD FOR ALL YOUR SIN – NEVER MIND!

The stage fills with yellow gas.

VOICE OFF Gas! Gas! Gas!

*The music hall fills with gas. The lights go down on
the fantasy world and come up on the trench. We see
ROBERTS staggering, and frantically trying to pull on
his gas mask. He is helped by another figure already
wearing a gas mask...*

Blackout.

Scene Eleven

Field hospital.

The music fades and we see PEARSON *talking to a* NURSE.

PEARSON I've come to see Captain Roberts. How is he?

NURSE Very bad.

PEARSON Oh dear.

NURSE I mean he's a very bad man. Disruptive, argumentative and keeps making the most appalling jokes.

PEARSON That's Fred for you.

NURSE I've had to tell Captain Roberts that this is NOT the palace of varieties!

PEARSON And what did he say?

NURSE He said, "No. The girls here are much better looking!"

NURSE *embarrassed but flattered.*

PEARSON Sounds like he's on the mend!

ROBERTS *enters in a wheelchair. He is frail, but reading the paper which has now become* The New Church Times *incorporating* The Wipers Times.

Fred! Good to see you! How are you?

ROBERTS Fighting fit. And ready to be as offensive as possible.

PEARSON So you got the paper?

ROBERTS *(weakly)* Looks capital, Jack, Tyler and his devils have done a fine job.

ROBERTS *coughs and retches.* NURSE *gets him glass of water.*

Nothing to worry about, Jack. Quacks say they'll have me right as rain and back on the front line in no time.

PEARSON Really?

ROBERTS I was lucky. It appears Fritz has developed a new type of stink bomb – makes you retch so you have to take off your gas mask and then the chlorine kills you.

PEARSON Fiendish...

ROBERTS *coughs.*

Are you sure you're all right?

ROBERTS Absolutely. Quacks say they'll have me right as rain and back on the front line in no time.

PEARSON Well you'd better be smart about it because apparently the war is going to be over within the week!

ROBERTS Says who?

PEARSON Says Hilaire Belloc.

ROBERTS *holds up copy of an article in the magazine Land and Water.*

ROBERTS Oh. Didn't he say the war was going to be over within the week last week?

PEARSON I rather think he did.

ROBERTS And the week before?

PEARSON You're just jealous because we haven't got our own expert on the war, someone who knows what is **really** going on.

ROBERTS Yes, you're right. We should employ one.

PEARSON *thinks.*

PEARSON How about Belary Helloc? I hear he is very well informed.

ROBERTS Really? So what is Mr Helloc's latest take on the war?

PEARSON I think his expert view is something along the lines of...

We switch to the fantasy world of the newspaper. A spotlight picks out one of the **MEN** *who wears a tweed* *jacket and holds a pipe becoming the very pompous* **HILAIRE BELLOC/BELARY HELLOC** *in front of a blackboard.*

HELLOC Good evening. I'm the famous Belary Helloc. And tonight my subject is: "Why we are going to win the war".

He goes to blackboard.

Everything points to a speedy disintegration of the enemy. Let us just look at the figures.

He writes all these figures on the blackboard as a mathematical sum.

There are twelve million fighting men in Germany. Of these, nine million are already killed or are being killed as we speak, leaving just three million...

We see him doing this on board.

Of these two million five hundred thousand are temperamentally unsuitable for fighting owing to obesity due to eating sausages. This leaves us five hundred thousand as the full German strength.

We see him doing this subtraction as he goes.

Of these four hundred and ninety-seven thousand, two hundred and fifty are suffering from incurable diseases – we all know which ones...

He taps his nose suggestively.

Leaving just two thousand seven hundred and fifty men. Of these, two thousand one hundred and fifty are on the Eastern Front. Of the remaining six hundred five hundred and eighty four are generals and staff.

He does subtraction again.

Thus we find that there are just... sixteen men on the Western Front.

This is the final flourish – we see the last figure sixteen on the board.

Clearly not enough to resist one final big push. Or maybe two. Or three. Four at the very most. And that is why we are going to win the war...if we haven't already won it while I've been talking.

ROBERTS Bravo!

Coughs again. **NURSE** *re-enters.*

NURSE Telegram for you, Captain Roberts.

ROBERTS Thank you.

A moment of flirtatious eye contact.

The service here Jack really is superb – you should try it!

He reads the telegram.

It's from General Mitford. I'm to be sent on leave.

NURSE Do I take it you're leaving us Captain Roberts?

ROBERTS I'm heartbroken, of course. Though I expect you'll be heartily glad to see the back of me.

NURSE Put it this way – I hope I never see you here again.

NURSE *smiles and exits.*

PEARSON Lucky fellow – spot of R and R behind the lines!

ROBERTS Though, I'll miss Wipers.

PEARSON Unlike the Boche artilery, which has made rather a mess of it.

ROBERTS Yes, I'm not altogether keen on their idea of landscape gardening.

PEARSON *shakes* **ROBERTS**'*s hand*

PEARSON Well enjoy yourself. And don't do anything silly.

ROBERTS Like what?

PEARSON Like...come back?

Song to cover scene change.

MEN

OH MADEMOISELLE CHÈRE MADEMOISELLE,
HOW BELLE YOU LOOK TODAY,
GIVE ME A KISS WITH THOSE SOFT
CHERRY LIPS, BEFORE I RETURN TO THE FRAY

OH MADEMOISELLE CHÈRE MADEMOISELLE,
COME FOR A NICE PROMENAY?
BUT IT'S ALWAYS THE SAME WITH YOUR
"APRES LA GUERRE"
AND YOUR "ME NO COMPRIS WHAT YOU
SAY".

Scene Twelve

French bar, night. French music plays. It is Madame Fifi's – with a candlelit table and chair. MADAME FIFI *has a bottle of champagne waiting.* ROBERTS, *on leave, enters with knapsack. He coughs throughout the scene.*

ROBERTS You must be Madame Fifi…

MADAME FIFI Bien sur.

(Flirting outrageously) And who are you, handsome soldier?

He sits at the table. She brings him champagne.

ROBERTS Me? Oh, I'm…er… Lieutenant Colonel Hector Alexander Howfield.

MADAME FIFI And your regiment?

ROBERTS *(coughs)* The um…um… Umpshires. The 17th/21st Umpshires…at your service.

MADAME FIFI And have you heard the rumours?

ROBERTS I have… I've heard that if I buy a bottle of champagne a beautiful girl will sit on my knee.

She comes and sits on his knee.

MADAME FIFI No, I meant rumours about the war.

ROBERTS What rumours?

MADAME FIFI You tell me.

ROBERTS Well apparently the Kaiser has gone to bed with a severe case of whooping cough and rickets.

MADAME FIFI You are joking.

ROBERTS No. The Germans have put wheels on their battleships and are sending them to the front line as tanks.

MADAME FIFI Be serious.

ROBERTS OK *(serious)* I have it on extremely good authority that the Pope is raising an army of nuns to come and stop the war.

MADAME FIFI You are laughing at me.

ROBERTS No, at myself. The war. Everything. *(He coughs again)*

We hear dance music start up.

MADAME FIFI Would you like to dance?

ROBERTS Absolutely! I'm an expert. I learned at Professor Dodgit's Dance Academy.

MADAME FIFI Professor...?

ROBERTS Surely you've heard of Professor Dodgit? He's internationally renowned! No more old fashioned sleepy dances. The prof teaches all the newest steps...like the Duckboard Dangle and the Whizz-Bang Hop.

He demonstrates, getting drunker and hurling himself around energetically.

Not forgetting the Crump Crawl and Machine Gun Slither.

MADAME FIFI *laughs at his mad gyrations.*

Courses are continuous day and night.

MADAME FIFI Will you teach me?

ROBERTS Naturellement! As Prof Dodgit says in the advertisement: "Come and learn to skip and hop, before you venture over the top"...

He is now on the floor, coughing from his exertions. The dancing is over.

MADAME FIFI Maybe in return I can give **you** some French lessons...

ROBERTS *(breathless)* That's jolly decent of you and to refuse seems ungentlemanly but however much I would love to take up your offer

MADAME FIFI What's the matter?

ROBERTS Can I tell you a secret?

MADAME FIFI Of course...

ROBERTS I don't think my wife would approve.

MADAME FIFI You are scared? The brave English soldier is frightened of Madame Fifi?

ROBERTS No! Well...yes.

He puts money down on the table.

I think I'd better be off. Got a war to win.

ROBERTS *bows to her, kisses her hand and leaves.*

Scene Thirteen

Editorial den. PEARSON *is listening to music correcting page proofs when* HENDERSON *enters with* TYLER.

TYLER Private Henderson to see you, sir. Tenshun!

PEARSON Yes, Henderson, I've been informed that last night on trench duty you failed to salute an officer.

HENDERSON It was dark, sir.

PEARSON You realise you could be court martialled?

HENDERSON And foggy, sir. I couldn't see his rank stars.

PEARSON The weather is no excuse, Henderson.

HENDERSON No, sir. But perhaps officers could assist in identifying themselves?

PEARSON How so? By having powerful electric lamps strapped to their shoulders to illuminate themselves?

HENDERSON That would help, sir.

PEARSON And it doesn't worry you that an officer wandering about looking like the Blackpool illuminations might be an easy target for the Hun?

HENDERSON *remains silent. He's not too bothered.*

TYLER Answer the officer.

HENDERSON I was wondering about the batteries for the lamps, sir, and where you'd carry them, and what...

PEARSON Yes all right Henderson! Next time you see an officer just stick to the damn regulations!

ROBERTS *enters.* HENDERSON *snaps to attention and salutes elaborately. He then stands to attention, wheels, salutes again. And then again.*

(Laughs) Sergeant, get Henderson out of here.

TYLER *and* SMITH *exit.* PEARSON *leaps up to shake* ROBERTS's *hand.*

ROBERTS Trouble, Jack?

PEARSON No, Henderson's just given me an idea for a piece. But more importantly how was leave?

ROBERTS Amiens really is most agreeable. Top notch cathedral which sadly I didn't have time to visit. But Madame Fifi assured me it's one of the finest examples of Gothic architecture in northern France.

PEARSON And Madame Fifi is...?

ROBERTS Absolutely charming. She runs the most delightful little club. You really must go there, Jack. In fact EVERYONE must go there. I'm giving all ranks one day's leave in Amiens!

PEARSON Well that'll be convenient.

ROBERTS Why?

PEARSON We've been posted nearby. I've received our orders. We're on the move again.

ROBERTS Excellent! You'll like it. It's very pretty indeed. Lovely river there.

PEARSON *looks at map with orders.*

PEARSON Oh yes. The Somme.

Song covers scene change.

MEN

NOW WE'RE HERE IN PASTURES NEW,
GIVING LESSONS THE HUN ONCE GAVE,
THE BEST OF LUCK TO ALL OF YOU
IN TEACHING FRITZ HOW TO BEHAVE.
WE CAN TAKE WHAT COMES ALONG,
WE'VE FOUGHT AND WORKED AND HELD
OUR LINE,
YOU'LL STILL FIND US GOING STRONG,
THE GAME'S AFOOT AND THE GOAL'S THE RHINE.

Scene Fourteen

Trench. The Somme.

ROBERTS and MEN in a trench preparing to go over the top. ROBERTS is reading a page proof of what we see is The Somme Times. *We hear the artillery barrage.*

PEARSON Zero minus five, Fred.

ROBERTS Sorry Jack, this issue is a bit thin. I am not sure we will be able to meet the deadline.

PEARSON We **have** had other calls on our time.

ROBERTS Perhaps we should wait and bring it out **after** the grand show?

A mortar explodes overhead.

PEARSON No – perhaps **sooner** would be better than later!

They look at each other and laugh. The barrage intensifies.

ROBERTS A harpsichord of hate performed to an audience of terrified Teutons...

PEARSON That's rather good...

ROBERTS Yes I must remember it if I get out of this...

He carries on looking at his page proofs.

(Whispers to PEARSON) Rum ration.

PEARSON Rum ration, sergeant. Is there time to give the boys a tot?

TYLER Sir!

TYLER passes a jug down the line, and the SOLDIERS tip it into their tin mugs.

BARNES Cheers, sarnt.

HENDERSON Dodd's too young – I'll have his.

TYLER We don't want you incapable, Henderson.

BARNES How would you tell, sarnt?

MEN laugh.

HENDERSON Any chance of seconds?

TYLER No – it's bad for your health.

A shell lands on the other side of the parapet, showering mud into everyone's mugs.

PEARSON Swine! Can't they even let a man enjoy a drink in peace!

DODD interrupts them. The other MEN are gathered nearby, sheltering in a line behind the wall of the trench. Being the most junior he has been put up to this by the others.

DODD Excuse me for asking, sir – but there's a rumour going round. Is this the big push?

ROBERTS I am afraid such information is a bit hush-hush, Dodd. Who told you that?

DODD The Germans, sir. They were shouting out across no man's land.

ROBERTS Yes, perhaps it is not the best-kept military secret in the history of the British Army...

Barrage really fierce.

TYLER Our boys are putting up quite a dump now!

PEARSON Zero minus three.

The MEN are gathering round, ready to go over the top.

ROBERTS OK men, I just wanted to say that whatever happens, we know that we can rely on the old division to give a good account of itself.

HENDERSON Even Dodd, Sir?

ROBERTS *(patting DODD on the shoulder)* Especially Dodd! So here's to all you lads! The game has started! Keep the ball rolling – and remember that the only good Hun is a dead Hun!

The **MEN** *cheer. Huge finale to barrage.* **ROBERTS** *stuffs proof pages into his uniform and gets out his whistle.*

PEARSON No jokes then?

ROBERTS Bit short on jokes.

The barrage stops and the **MEN** *look scared in the silence that follows. To reassure them* **ROBERTS** *begins...*

There was a young girl of the Somme, who sat on a number five bomb...

He looks to **PEARSON** *who continues the rhyme.*

PEARSON She thought twas a dud 'un, but it went off sudden...

ROBERTS Her exit she made with aplomb!

The **MEN** *laugh and cheer.* **ROBERTS** *blows the whistle. They go over the top.*

Blackout.

Interval

ACT TWO

Scene One

Mitford's office, divisional HQ.

GENERAL MITFORD *is reading very long casualty lists.*

MITFORD Renwick B... Reynolds F... Reynolds P... Richards J... Richards M... Richards T... Richardson L... Roach T... Robb G... Robbins D...

Enter **LIEUTENANT COLONEL HOWFIELD.**

HOWFIELD Did you know that it is still going on?

MITFORD The war? Yes, apparently it is...

HOWFIELD No – this mutinous magazine!

He brandishes a copy of the The Somme Times.

MITFORD They have promised to stop producing it as soon as the war is over...

HOWFIELD Just look at this.

He shows **MITFORD** *article and reads it out.*

"Realising that men must laugh some wise man devised the Staff". Is that supposed to be funny?

MITFORD Funnier than what I am reading...

HOWFIELD It's a subversive attack on the entire High Command. It continues: "Let them lead the simple life far from all our vulgar strife..." By God that's **us** they're talking about!

(He continues, angrily) "Lest their relatives might grieve often, often give them leave –

59

Decorations too galore What on earth could man wish more."

MITFORD *is smiling benevolently.*

We **cannot** allow this scurrilous insubordination to go unpunished!

MITFORD *(takes the paper and continues reading, finishing the rhyme)* "Yet alas, or so says the rumour, the Staff all lack a sense of humour".

There is a pause as this sinks in...

HOWFIELD Utter rubbish...

MITFORD And it's not all rude rhymes – in fact they have put in a rather helpful glossary of military terms.

HOWFIELD Really?

MITFORD Yes.

(He reads) "Duds. There are two kinds. A shell on impact failing to explode is called a dud. They are unhappily not as plentiful as the other kind of Dud".

HOWFIELD *(suspicious)* Go on.

MITFORD 'The kind that draws a big salary and explodes for no reason far behind the fighting area.'

HOWFIELD *(explodes)* The battlefield is not the place for humour!

MITFORD Humour, my dear Howfield, is what separates civilization from incivility. Us from the Boche.

While Roberts and his merry men are writing poems poking fun at us brass hats – the German's equivalent literary contribution is a "Hymn of Hate". Have you heard it?

HOWFIELD Of course I have heard it.

MITFORD It has all the subtlety of a dawn barrage from Big Bertha.

HOWFIELD What the Germans sing or don't sing is irrelevant. We have to maintain discipline in our army or the result is defeatism and anarchy!

MITFORD Really? What do our chaps sing as they march along? Is it "Rule Britannia?" Is it "God Save The King"?

HOWFIELD No, not generally...

MITFORD No, they sing "It's a long way to Tipperary" – which is a comic music hall song about a lovelorn and quite possibly drunk Irishman who wants to go home to his sweetheart. Is that defeatist? Is that anarchic? Or does it keep the poor bloody infantry going through the mud? Tommy Atkins decides what he sings, what he finds funny and whether or not he wants to win the bloody war!

Pause as **HOWFIELD** *is silenced.*

HOWFIELD Is still say that something should be done about Captain Roberts.

MITFORD Something has been done.

MITFORD *hands* **HOWFIELD** *a citation.*

He has been awarded the Military Cross for Gallantry.

On the other side of the stage, in **ROBERTS**'s *den,* **ROBERTS** *looks embarrassed as* **PEARSON** *and the* **MEN** *shake his hand, and pat him on the back.*

(voiceover) Captain FJ Roberts, 12th Sherwood Foresters, 24th Division. For conspicuous bravery, gallantry and devotion to duty in the battle of the Somme on August 12th 1916 Captain Roberts showed outstanding leadership under fire as company commander. Throughout he behaved most bravely.

ROBERTS *packs his bed roll and knapsack and exits on leave.*

Song covers scene change.

MEN
IF YOU'RE WAKING CALL ME EARLY,

CALL ME EARLY SERGEANT DEAR.
FOR I'M VERY, VERY WEARY,
AND MY WARRANT'S COME, I HEAR;
IT'S "BLIGHTY" FOR A SPELL,
AND MY OLD TROUBLES ARE ALL PACKED,
SO KEEP THE WAR A'GOING SARGE,
IT'S ALL YOURS UNTIL I'M BACK!

Scene Two

The Ritz dining room.

We see **ROBERTS** *on leave with his wife* **KATE** *in the opulent splendour of the Ritz restaurant. A string quartet plays. He is wearing his smartest uniform with MC medal ribbon. He waves his napkin.*

ROBERTS Mâitre d'! More of...**everything**!

KATE *laughs.* **ROBERTS** *tucks into the beef and drinks his claret enthusiastically. Maitre D' tops up their glasses.*

Pearson is priceless, and Tyler is an ace with the inkies and you'd be amazed at the sort of stuff that comes in from the chaps' spoofs of Kipling and Sherlock Homes and the Rubiyat of Omar Whatsit and limericks and jokes from all sorts of unlikely coves...

KATE Slow down Fred, I am not going anywhere!

ROBERTS Have I told you about the poet Gilbert Frankau contributing? Now there's someone who's actually famous and now he is working for us!

KATE Yes, you did mention it Fred...once or twice...

ROBERTS And there's a very promising writer called Sherrif who's good at little dramatic squibs and now one of the men has started carving drawings on wood-blocks – so we're almost up there with the Illustrated London News...

KATE You make it all sound such fun...

ROBERTS It would be – but the infernal General Staff do keep insisting on us fighting all the time...But enough of me. Tell me about the chickens. Are they still engaged in vital war work?

KATE They most certainly are. Did you know that on the black market eggs are now four pence each?

ROBERTS Good heavens!

KATE If our chickens weren't donating their services to charity, they'd be driving around in a Rolls Royce.

ROBERTS But then they wouldn't be making a noble sacrifice.

KATE And they'd be suspected of being shirkers.

ROBERTS Some high minded lady might present our brave chicks with a white feather....

KATE And accuse them of being...chicken! *They both dissolve into laughter.*

ROBERTS I thought producing terrible puns was my job!

KATE With the men away the women have to assume all sorts of roles...bus drivers, munitions workers...

ROBERTS ...bad joke makers... whatever next? I propose a toast – to women – and particularly to my darling wife!

They clink glasses.

(Calls off, waving bottle) I say sommelier! Another bottle of the 97!

MAITRE D' Very good choice Sir. It's particularly...

ROBERTS Expensive? Excellent!

KATE *(laughing)* Darling, are you sure we can afford this?

ROBERTS Of course we can't! Not on a captain's pay. But as luck would have it I ran into a general on the boat home and won a hand or two at cards. I do hope he is better at strategy than he is at bridge...

KATE *is giggling.*

KATE Same old Fred!

ROBERTS *(more rueful)* Not quite.

He is still smiling but the smile is strained. The mood has changed.

KATE What's it really like?

ROBERTS Do you know what the basis of this war is? Mud. And sticking through the mud at various places you can see pieces of towns. And out there are the trenches – one set for our men and one for the Boche with thick wire fences in front of them.

KATE *holds his hand.*

The time passes slowly and by way of amusement one side or the other will try and get into the other trenches and bring back a man. And then the score is one-nil for the night. It may seem a bit slow taking the enemy one by one as there are millions more out there, but it all helps to pass the time until Christmas when the war is going to end.

KATE Is it?

ROBERTS Oh yes. We just don't know **which** Christmas.

KATE Aren't you afraid?

ROBERTS *(smiling cheerfully)* Of course I'm afraid. Of the thirty-two of our officers who left Blighty after training, just seven of us have survived. But I'm more afraid of **not** being killed.

KATE What?

ROBERTS I'm afraid of coming back to you as a bloody hulk that you have to look after for the rest of your life. Half a man.

KATE Half of you would be twice as good as other men.

ROBERTS *kisses her hand.*

ROBERTS Now you are talking nonsense Kate. That really is my job.

KATE But we are winning?

ROBERTS I am not sure anyone knows. I fought in a battle which was an epic of futility. No-one could even speculate what the battle was supposed to achieve. In fact there was never the slightest chance of it achieving anything. Apart from the flower of British manhood being hurled to a squalid death.

KATE This isn't like you, Fred.

ROBERTS I'm sorry. Most of us have been cured of any illusions we may have had about the pomp and the glory of war and now know it for the vilest disaster that can befall mankind. War is nothing more than wallowing in a dirty ditch.

KATE Are you going back?

ROBERTS Of course.

Song covers scene change.

MEN
IN THE LINE A SOLDIER'S FANCY,
OFT MAY TURN TO THOUGHTS OF LOVE
BUT ITS HARD TO DREAM OF NANCY,
WHEN THE WHIZZ-BANGS SING ABOVE.

DON'T DREAM WHEN NEAR MACHINE GUNS,
PUT NANCY OUT OF MIND,
JUST THINK OF THOSE UNSEEN HUNS,
A SNIPER'S QUICK AND LOVE IS BLIND.

Scene Three

ROBERTS*'s new den.* PEARSON *is correcting proofs.*

ROBERTS *enters with bag. He is back from leave.*

ROBERTS Anyone home?

PEARSON Fred – how good to see you!

ROBERTS Ah! *Frère Jacques! Bonjour!*

PEARSON How was London? See any good shows?

ROBERTS We took in the Bunny Sisters, thought we could call them the Hun-y sisters and – good lord, Jack, what've you done to yourself?

He goes to shake PEARSON*'s hand – but it is heavily bandaged.*

PEARSON *(shrugs)* Oh it's nothing really.

I was sent on a munitions course. Blew myself up.

ROBERTS I'm a bit rusty after all that leave – but isn't the idea to blow the Germans up?

PEARSON Got my wires crossed. Quite literally, as it happens.

ROBERTS Should you even be here?

PEARSON Of course! Wouldn't want to miss all the fun!

They look at each other wryly.

ROBERTS Back home all the papers are full of our historic victory at the Somme.

PEARSON Was it? I don't remember that bit.

ROBERTS How many did the brigade lose?

PEARSON Too many.

ROBERTS *(pause)* What about Henderson... They seemed hopeful. Did he... (make it)?

Sadly, PEARSON *shakes his head.*

I'm so very sorry.

PEARSON The damned idiocy is that Henderson didn't die of his wounds – which were horrendous enough – but of dehydration. It's somewhat ironic that in a sea of mud and a deluge of rain a soldier should die of thirst.

A moment of grief. Enter **TYLER**.

TYLER Welcome back, sir. I thought you should see these.

He produces a large sack of mail.

More submissions, sir.

ROBERTS Excellent!

PEARSON You haven't read them, Fred.

ROBERTS Please tell me it isn't all poetry.

PEARSON Fine – it isn't all poetry. But that's a lie. It **is** all poetry.

ROBERTS Damn and blast! Alert the medical orderlies at once, Jack. We have an outbreak of poetitis!

PEARSON Subalterns have been seen with a notebook in one hand and bomb in the other absently walking near the wire in deep communion with the muse.

ROBERTS It's probably because spring is in the air.

PEARSON The picture of little lambs gambolling among the whizz-bangs is so beautiful and romantic.

ROBERTS I thought I'd made it clear that I have had enough of verse.

PEARSON You did, and our famous bard Mr Frankau has responded with a letter to the editor.

PEARSON finds letter.

ROBERTS Good, a letter. Honest-to-goodness prose. What does Gilbert have to say?

PEARSON *(reading)* The editor of *The Wipers Times* is, I gather sick of rhymes

ROBERTS Quite right.

PEARSON The best of reasons I suppose that I should henceforth stick to prose.

ROBERTS Hang on!

PEARSON No more I'll sing how transports wait, bi-nightly at the Menin Gate whilst some unthinking driver sits well in effective range of Fritz and galls his mules and smokes and spits...

ROBERTS Damn his impudence. That's a poem.

PEARSON Yes I rather think it is. Cleverly disguised as an obliging epistle. He continues:

PEARSON *reads the letter again.*

Verse was alright when we were pent in that unkindly salient. But now poetry has had its day, says the editor who does not pay.

ROBERTS *(laughs and splutters)* That's mutiny.

PEARSON What are you going to do about it?

ROBERTS Publish it in full.

PEARSON Quite right.

ROBERTS Are there any letters of a less critical nature?

PEARSON *has a sheaf of papers with him.*

PEARSON Er...no. There's a chap here who wants to know why on earth we don't write about the war?

ROBERTS I rather thought we did.

PEARSON No, the wider war, the big picture, the next Great Advance. Will it be as successful as the last Great Advance?

ROBERTS I do hope not!

PEARSON Are we going to be in Berlin by tomorrow?

ROBERTS *chuckles.*

ROBERTS We can't write about the wider war because we've no idea what's going on. We're just fighting it.

PEARSON Well it's a good thing we've got illustrious war correspondents like William Beach Thomas to keep us informed.

PEARSON passes a copy of the Daily Mail to **ROBERTS**, *who splutters in indignation.*

ROBERTS Beach Thomas? That idiot?

PEARSON No, he is highly respected because he always manages to write from the thick of the action.

Beat.

Funny how we've never actually seen him.

ROBERTS I prefer our own correspondent. Teach Bomas.

PEARSON Yes, he's awfully good!

The two **MEN** *grab pen and paper.*

ROBERTS *(dictating in pompous voice)* I'm here in no man's land where all hell is breaking loose...

French accordion music strikes up, as the spotlight picks out one of the **MEN** *who wears a silly moustache to become the pompous war correspondent Beach Thomas sitting at a bar with a bottle of wine and a typewriter. Another of the* **MEN** *becomes a waiter. We are in the magazine's fantasy sketch.*

BOMAS I'm here in no mans land where all hell is breaking loose...

He takes a swig of his glass of wine.

...the air is thick with bullets and shells – but I don't mind that – and now I am climbing up a conveniently dangling rope into an observation balloon.

He narrates as he types.

...and I am now right above the battle witnessing the gallant charge of the... *(Tries to think of the name of a regiment)*... Blankshires, yes it's the men of the 13th Blankshire Regiment charging straight at the elite Prussian Guard...who are all surrendering, yes they are shouting "Kamerad" and putting up their hands.

He raises his hands to click for a waiter to bring more wine.

I am now sailing over the German lines, and I can tell you with complete authority that the cavalry are laying down a barrage of shells whilst the submarines advance into the wood...

Waiter tops up his glass.

This has been me, William Teach Bomas, writing exclusively from the middle of the bottle...sorry, battle.

Music stops, spotlight fades and we are back in the den.

PEARSON *(chuckling, as he reads)* Come on Fred, you're being cynical. Teach Bomas must know what he is talking about. He's in the Daily Mail!

ROBERTS Now who is being cynical?

PEARSON Does Mr Bomas have any inside knowledge as to where we are off to next?

ROBERTS No, he's very good on the North Southshires being deployed on the Blindenberg line but he's not got much idea where the 24th Division is going...

PEARSON Does anyone know what's going on?

ROBERTS Not even the Cabinet. Apparently Kitchener won't tell them anything for fear they'll tell their wives. Or in Lloyd George's case, someone else's wife.

PEARSON Careful Fred. That sounds like a contravention of The Defence of the Realm Act. That joke could be undermining the morale of His Majesty's forces and the civilian population.

ROBERTS *laughs.* **BARNES** *appears shyly at the door.*

ROBERTS Hello Barnes! What is it?

BARNES *(salutes)* Sir. I was just wondering – are you still taking submissions for *The Wipers Times*?

PEARSON So long as it isn't poetry. The editor has decided that he is sick of rhyme. *(Quoting* **ROBERTS***)* "A paper cannot live by poems alone."

ROBERTS Quite so!

BARNES Oh.

ROBERTS So what do you have for me?

BARNES Nothing, sir.

ROBERTS Show me, Barnes.

> **PEARSON** *holds out his hand and takes a bit of paper and starts reading.*

"To My Chum". Looks suspiciously like a poem to me.

BARNES It's about Henderson, sir.

ROBERTS Ah, in this case we might make a bit of an exception...

Scene Four

BARNES *begins reciting his poem in a spotlight, as we see the shapes of a burial party on stage, lit up by the occasional flare. We see them marching out, digging, shovelling earth onto the body, listening to the padre mouthing words we cannot hear, putting a makeshift cross in the ground and then marching back again.*

Maybe we see all this in silhouette. Or animated on screen.

BARNES *(voiceover)* No more we'll share the same old barn,

The same old dug-out, same old yarn,

No more a tin of bully share, nor split our rum by a star-shell's glare, so long old lad.

What times we've had, both good and bad,

We've shared what shelter could be had,

The same crump-hole when the whizz-bangs shrieked,

The same old billet that always leaked, and now – you've "stopped one".

We'd weathered the storms two winters long,

We'd managed to grin when all went wrong,

Because together we fought and fed,

Our hearts were light; but now – you're dead,

And I am mateless.

At the end of the poem, the burial party stand solemnly – until they too are shelled and run for cover.

Scene Five

The **MEN**, *led by* **ROBERTS**, *march round in a circle. On the screen we see a succession of bombed-out landscapes that all look the same.*

TYLER Section halt!

The **MEN** *fall out for cigarette break.*

PEARSON *and* **ROBERTS** *are consulting a map.*

DODD Where are we, sir? Are we in Berlin?

PEARSON Not quite yet. If I am not mistaken we are back in Wipers.

They all look at landscape.

DODD Are you sure, sir?

PEARSON *picks up a pock-marked road sign saying "Ypres".*

PEARSON Pretty sure.

ROBERTS We've come a long way in the last eighteen months haven't we, Jack?

PEARSON *consults map.*

PEARSON I make it approximately thirty yards.

Pause.

ROBERTS Sergeant?

TYLER Sir?

ROBERTS Make sure the printer has made it in one piece. That GS wagon we put it on looked pretty ropey.

TYLER Yes sir.

ROBERTS And who the devil is that?

A well dressed **FRENCH PHOTOGRAPHER** *in a boater enters, sets up his camera tripod and equipment and* *takes a picture. When the flash goes and we hear a pop, on the back screen appears the picture he is taking which is of the stump of the Cloth Hall in Ypres in 1917 even more bombed out than ever.*

ROBERTS *tries to engage the* **PHOTOGRAPHER** *in faltering French...*

Monsieur...*qu'est-ce que vous*...are up to?

The **PHOTOGRAPHER** *looks confused but reaches in his coat for his papers and shows them to* **ROBERTS***.*

PHOTOGRAPHER *J'ai tous les documents officiels necessaires.*

ROBERTS Lieutenant Pearson, help me out here.

PEARSON *(fluent) Pardon monsieur, le capitaine veut dire que c'est tres dangereux ici...*

PHOTOGRAPHER *Oui je comprends tout ca, mais j'ai les permissions pour prendre des photographes pour le guide Michelin...*

PHOTOGRAPHER *points to paper where it is all explained.*

PEARSON *Vraiment! C'est incroyable...*

ROBERTS Fill me in, Lieutenant.

PEARSON I don't think you are going to believe this, sir.

ROBERTS Try me.

PEARSON He's from the Michelin guides. They are preparing a tourist handbook of the battlefields.

PHOTOGRAPHER *Oui, certainement, c'est une idee tres commerciale...*

ROBERTS So this is going to be a holiday destination.

PEARSON Apparently so. *(Pause)* We should consider ourselves fortunate to be among the first to have seen the sights.

ROBERTS Could you ask our holiday guide if he could recommend any top-class restaurants in the vicinity?

They look at the bombed-out landscape.

PEARSON *(aside)* This is beyond parody, Fred. You couldn't make this up.

ROBERTS *(aside)* They'll be putting *The Wipers Times* out of business.

ROBERTS *hands the* **PHOTOGRAPHER** *back his papers.*

Merci monsieur! Carryez-vous on!

PEARSON Very good, sir. You speak like a native...of Borneo.

ROBERTS Thank you. So shall we see if our old editorial den has survived? Is the Hotel Des Ramparts still open?

PEARSON It'll be just like old times.

ROBERTS Very old times – before they had any buildings at all.

Scene Six

It begins to snow. We hear a Christmas "carol".

CAROL

SING A SONG OF CHRISTMAS,
POCKETS FULL OF SLUSH,
FOUR AND TWENTY SOLDIERS
A COOKPOT FULL OF MUSH
AND WHEN THE POT WAS OPENED
THE TOMMIES SAID "OH MY!"
IT'S BEEF TODAY BY WAY OF CHANGE
AND THEN BEGAN TO CRY

ROBERTS *and* **PEARSON** *in their old den. A sign says "Hotel Des Ramparts. Special Christmas Menu". There is an attempt at Christmas decoration. A shell-shot tree stump has a star placed upon it. There is also evidence of magazine production with proofs up on walls, type and blocks laid out.* **ROBERTS** *is in the middle of writing a piece for* The Wipers Times. *When the shell explodes nearby, the building shakes but they pay no attention they are so used to it by this stage of the war.*

ROBERTS Tell me, sergeant, how many "e"s in Wenceslas?

TYLER As many of the little blighters as I can find, sir. Which at the moment is none.

ROBERTS Very good. I always thought the good king was over-encumbered with "e"s.

TYLER We are also short of paper, sir.

ROBERTS But we have a bumper Christmas issue to produce!

PEARSON I'm sure the readers will understand if the issue contains less than the advertised twenty pages then we've had to drop the pen for the sword.

ROBERTS No, we've promised our readers twenty pages and twenty pages they shall have!

TYLER That's all well and good, Sir, but it doesn't get round our problem. Napoo paper.

ROBERTS If I can find something funny to say about another
Christmas on the front line, Sergeant, then I am sure **you**
can find some paper somewhere in Ypres.

ROBERTS *hands* TYLER *some banknotes.*

Thank you.

TYLER I'll do my best, sir.

TYLER *checks in the doorway for shells overhead and
then exits at a run.*

ROBERTS *(to* PEARSON*)* Had a rather profitable game of Bridge
with Bobbing Bobby.

PEARSON *laughs.*

PEARSON If this issue comes out at all it will be a miracle.

ROBERTS *thinks, puts pen to paper and begins to write.*

ROBERTS *(narrating as he writes)* A miracle at Christmas. This
is the story of a soldier, Alfred Higgins, or Number 249,921
Private Higgins, A – as he was officially known.

The light fades on ROBERTS *and picks out* DODD *as*
HIGGINS *in a trench in the snow. We are in the fantasy
world of* ROBERTS*'s imagination. The sound of God Rest
You Merry Gentlemen is drifting across no man's land.*

(voiceover) It was Christmas morning and Alfred was
holding the line. All was peace and goodwill. The gas gongs
were chiming out their message of joy to all mankind...

We see BARNES *and* SMITH *wearing masks ringing gas
bells.*

(voiceover) ...and the merry bark of the pipsqueak aided by
the staccato cough of the howitzer combined to reassure
Alfred that all was well with the world...

HIGGINS/DODD *looks very scared and flinches as bangs
and crumps fill the air. And the weariness kicks in...*

(voiceover) Alfred began to doze...when at last his sergeant came in sight...

We see **TYLER** *looking fierce as a* **SERGEANT** *approaching* **HIGGINS/DODD.**

(voiceover) ..."Higgins", said the sergeant. "Have you been drinking rum?"...

We see this mimed out by the **MEN.**

(voiceover) ..."No sergeant, honestly sergeant!" said Higgins...

(voiceover) "Well then," said the sergeant, "you must have some of mine".

We see **SERGEANT/TYLER** *cheerily hand over his flagon.* **HIGGINS/DODD** *faints with shock.*

(voiceover) Alfred was treated for severe shock and never went to the front line again.

We see **HIGGINS/DODD** *beaming with attractive nurse who is tending to him...*

A happy Christmas and new year to all and may next Christmas see the whole **damned** business over.

Lighting change and we are back in the den. **PEARSON** *is laughing at* **ROBERT**'s *copy.*

PEARSON Bravo Fred! A festive tale to gladden the heart. And it's given me an idea. Permission to go into the pub business.

ROBERTS Permission granted. What on earth are you talking about?

Song covers scene change.

MEN
THEY SAY LOVE MAKES THE WORLD GO ROUND,
BUT I DO NOT AGREE
IT WAS RUM NOT LOVE I HAD LAST NIGHT,
THAT MADE THE WHOLE WORLD SPIN ROUND ME.

Scene Seven

HQ Arras. **HOWFIELD** *and* **MITFORD** *and* **TEMPERANCE LADY**.

LADY SOMERSBY I hardly need to tell you, General Mitford, that it is an incontestable fact that alcohol is undermining the war effort. Drink is doing more damage in the war than all the German submarines put together.

MITFORD *has been pouring drinks from a decanter. He pours them back again surreptitiously.*

HOWFIELD Absolutely, Lady Somersby, and we are very sympathetic to the views of the Temperance Society.

MITFORD Though the soldiers may be less sympathetic to the idea of losing their rum ration.

LADY SOMERSBY The rum ration is a disgrace!

MITFORD The men are in total agreement. They think it should be much larger and issued more frequently.

LADY SOMERSBY General Mitford, your army is drinking itself to defeat!

MITFORD Some of our medical officers are of the opinion that drinking is saving us from defeat.

HOWFIELD Ha ha. You must forgive General Mitford. He has become somewhat infected by trench humour.

LADY SOMERSBY Yes, I gather this awful trench periodical promotes the abuse of alcohol on every page!

HOWFIELD We do of course realise the severity of the alcohol crisis.

MITFORD Though I'm not sure it hasn't been somewhat exaggerated in some quarters.

LADY SOMERSBY Are you including in that suggestion Mr David Lloyd George who is not only Prime Minister but also a very good friend of mine?

MITFORD It must be most rewarding to be so close to the seat of power.

LADY SOMERSBY *doesn't get the innuendo.*

LADY SOMERSBY It is indeed...and Mr Lloyd George, specifically said, "We are fighting Germany, Austria and Drink. And the greatest of these foes is Drink"!

MITFORD He was of course speaking from his unique vantage point on the home front...

LADY SOMERSBY Perhaps you do not feel yourself answerable to the Prime Minister, General Mitford?

The atmosphere has turned nasty.

MITFORD I am always...

LADY SOMERSBY Then what about the King? His Majesty himself has set a noble example. He has risen to the high occasion and done the kingliest act of his reign. He has decided to give up alcohol for the good of his country, for the safety of the Empire.

HOWFIELD Very laudable. A fine sacrifice indeed.

LADY SOMERSBY The Russians have gone even further and introduced prohibition for the entire country

MITFORD I believe they have also had a revolution.

HOWFIELD Rest assured we will do everything in our power to support the admirable work of your society in trying to combat this deadly menace.

LADY SOMERSBY I am glad to hear it. As indeed will be my very very dear friend Mr Lloyd George. When I report back to him, I shall tell him Lieutenant Colonel Howfield was particularly receptive to his wishes.

She smiles at **MITFORD**.

Good day.

She exits.

MITFORD (*To* **HOWFIELD**) I don't know about you but I could do
with a drink.

Song covers the scene change

MEN

TEN FAT GERMANS WENT TO LAY A MINE
ONE LIT A CIGARETTE AND THEN THERE WERE NINE
NINE FAT GERMANS MARCHING TO THEIR FATE
ONE STOPPED A WHIZZ-BANG AND THEN THERE WERE EIGHT
EIGHT FAT GERMANS DREAMING HARD OF HEAVEN
ONE CAUGHT A FLYING PIG AND THEN THERE WERE SEVEN
SEVEN FAT GERMANS WORKING HARD WITH PICKS
ONE PICKED HIS NEIGHBOUR OFF AND THEN THERE WERE SIX...

Scene Eight

BARNES *and* **DODD** *roll a barrel across the stage and put up a sign which reads "The Forester's Arms". Another reads "Abandon rank all ye who enter here".*

PEARSON *(raising tankard)* Bienvenu and welcome to The Forester's Arms!

A cheer from the **MEN**. **ROBERTS** *looks on appreciatively*

What do you think, sir?

ROBERTS Very cosy, I must say!

PEARSON Something had to be done. Especially after poor Henderson. The ambulances can't keep pace with the casualties and get the wounded back to base quick enough. So this is a sort of first aid post.

ROBERTS Or rather thirst aid post.

PEARSON That's terrible, sir.

ROBERTS I do apologise. It's been a long war.

PEARSON Next!

PEARSON serves a bandaged **SOLDIER** *a drink.*

That will be a franc.

PEARSON gestures towards a tankard with some coins in it.

WOUNDED SOLDIER I haven't any money, sir.

PEARSON Then I'm very sorry, I will have no alternative but to give it to you for free.

SOLDIER Cheers, sir.

ROBERTS Ever the hardened businessman.

PEARSON You'd be surprised how many of them insist on paying, for each other as well as themselves. We use the profits to provide free soup and bread.

ROBERTS This seems incredibly efficient. I hope the Staff don't get to hear of it.

ROBERTS *orders drink.*

I'll have a pint please barman. And one for all my friends.

He puts note in the tankard. What **MEN** *there are raise a cheer.*

The staff officer, **LIEUTENANT COLONEL HOWFIELD** *appears.*

I spoke too soon!

HOWFIELD What the bloody hell is going on here? *(To* **PEARSON***)* You're meant to be a soldier not a bloody publican!

PEARSON We are just...

HOWFIELD I want it closed down immediately.

He hands **ROBERTS** *an order sheet.*

PEARSON But, sir! Perhaps we could refer this to General Mitford...?

HOWFIELD This comes straight from the High Command! We are cracking down on the excess of alcohol at the front. You will not be allowed to reinforce the impression that the trenches are awash with drink!

DRUNKEN SOLDIER Wahey!

HOWFIELD Shut up... *(turning to* **ROBERTS***)* So close it down! Now!

PEARSON *looks at* **ROBERTS** *who reluctantly nods.*

ROBERTS You heard the lieutenant colonel, Pearson.

HOWFIELD And it's not the only thing I'd like to close down!

HOWFIELD *exits.*

ROBERTS Tactical retreat, Jack. The good ladies of the Temperance Society have clearly won over the brass hats.

Whether we like it or not we will have to acknowledge that drink is a serious issue.

PEARSON So what do you propose?

ROBERTS Obviously we will have to do our bit and put in a suitable advertisement in a responsible trench newspaper.

We are in the world of **ROBERTS***'s imagination. One of the* **MEN** *is at a lectern addressing what appears to be a temperance meeting.*

DOCTOR *(to imaginary members of audience)* Do you have a drink habit? Do you have a drink habit? Do you have a drink habit? If not, I can help you acquire one in three days! If you or any one you know does not drink alcohol regularly, they need my new book – "Confessions of an Alcohol Slave"! I can cure anyone! Take this once-sad wretch...

He introduces DRUNK, *clearly in his cups.*

DRUNK I was a rabid teetotaller for the first 15 years of my life. But thanks to Doctor Supitup and his miracle cure I now never go to bed sober.

DOCTOR All cases will be treated in absolute confidence. This incredible three-step guide to being a bona fide toper is yours now – just write to me, Dr Supitup at Havanotha Mansions in Bedfordshire.

Meeting all cheers.

Lighting switches us back to The Forester's Arms.

WOUNDED SOLDIER One for my mate please sir!

PEARSON On the house!

Enter **LIEUTENANT COLONEL HOWFIELD.**

HOWFIELD Pearson, what the devil do you think is going on?

PEARSON Obeying orders, sir.

HOWFIELD I ordered you to shut this establishment down!

CHAPLAIN *(O.S.)* I'm afraid that's not possible.

HOWFIELD What!?

A **CHAPLAIN** *appears from behind the bar. He has clearly been serving and tending the wounded.*

CHAPLAIN The Forester's Arms is providing a vital service to these men and following a petition from the Divisional Chaplaincies The Forester's Arms has been authorised to continue its essential work.

He hands over order sheet.

HOWFIELD On whose authority? Field Marshall Haig's? The King's?

CHAPLAIN Higher than that.

CHAPLAIN *looks skywards.*

HOWFIELD You bloody Amen wallahs are going to undermine the whole war...

HOWFIELD *is further annoyed as* **ROBERTS** *enters and salutes.*

ROBERTS Glad it's all sorted, sir!

HOWFIELD Dammit Roberts – first you're comedians, now you're barmen – what next?

ROBERTS I was rather hoping to be a civilian, sir.

HOWFIELD You haven't heard the last of this, Roberts!

HOWFIELD *storms off.*

ROBERTS May I add my own note of caution Captain Pearson. I hope this new venture – however admirable – will not get in the way of your duties. May I remind you that you are first and foremost...the assistant editor of *The Wipers Times*.

TYLER *enters.*

TYLER Orders from HQ, sir. You have to present yourself at once.

ROBERTS *(to* **PEARSON***)* That's not usually good, is it?

PEARSON No. One for the road?

ROBERTS *exits.*

Song covers the scene change

MEN

SIX FAT GERMANS GLAD TO BE ALIVE
ONE WAS SENT TO VERDUN AND THEN
THERE WERE FIVE.
FIVE FAT GERMANS DIDN'T LIKE THE WAR
ONE SHOUTED KAMARAD AND THEN THERE WERE FOUR
FOUR FAT GERMANS TRIED TO FELL A TREE
ONE FELLED HIMSELF INSTEAD AND THEN THERE WERE THREE.
THREE FAT GERMANS FEELING VERY BLUE
ONE TRIED TO STOP A TANK AND THEN THERE WERE TWO...

Scene Nine

MITFORD*'s office HQ.* MITFORD *is looking at map as* ROBERTS *knocks and enters.*

MITFORD Fred! Come in!

ROBERTS *salutes, then removes his hat.*

ROBERTS If it's about The Forester's Arms, sir, I can explain...

MITFORD It isn't...

ROBERTS ...or about ragging the Temperance Society then...

MITFORD Not that either. Though you and Pearson have been sailing very close to the wind. There may come a point beyond which I can't help you.

ROBERTS Then we'll just have to rely on Divine intervention sir.

MITFORD *(chuckles)* Do be careful, Fred. Your version of the war does seem to consist of nothing but wine, women and song.

ROBERTS I confess there has been the odd visit to Madam Fifi's...

MITFORD I'd keep quiet about that, Fred, if I were you. Madam Fifi's has closed.

ROBERTS Napoo Madame Fifi! Quelle domage!

MITFORD Sadly she had to leave her cosy little club one dawn to keep an appointment with a firing squad.

ROBERTS Madam Fifi was a **spy**?

MITFORD Apparently she was extracting information from excitable young officers and passing it straight on to Berlin.

MITFORD *looks at* ROBERTS *meaningfully.*

ROBERTS My conscience is clear, sir. I can't have given anything away about the war because I don't know anything. Like all British officers on the front line I am kept completely in the dark.

MITFORD *(laughs)* Frankly I am amazed that after all this time you can still find anything funny.

ROBERTS Oh I don't know, sir...

He looks at map of Ypres above **MITFORD***'s desk.*

You would have to concede that it **is** somewhat comical that we have spent years fighting our way through Flanders only to end up...right back where we started.

MITFORD Then you're going to find the news of your next deployment hilarious...

ROBERTS I can hardly wait, sir.

MITFORD 24th Division is being sent back...to the Somme.

ROBERTS And why not, sir? It was such a success last time! Why not do it all again?

MITFORD That's the spirit! The war's waking up! Seconds out of the ring – last round coming up!

ROBERTS So see you for breakfast on the Unter den Linden!

Continuation of song covers scene change.

MEN

TWO FAT GERMANS WALKED INTO A GUN
THE GUNNER PULLED THE TRIGGER AND THEN THERE WAS ONE
ONE FAT GERMAN ALONE WITHOUT HIS MEN
ANOTHER NINE RECRUITS ARRIVED AND THEN THERE WERE TEN

The song starts up again .

MEN

TEN FAT GERMANS, COMING DOWN THE LINE..

Scene Ten

ROBERTS *and his* MEN *are about to launch yet another weary attack and go over the top.*

PEARSON Zero minus two.

ROBERTS OK men...you know the drill by now.

ROBERTS *tries to break the tension.*

And sergeant, I've some good news.

TYLER Sir?

ROBERTS All the men are to receive chevrons.

DODD What's a chevron, sir?

PEARSON It's a small v-shaped piece of coloured cloth to be sewn onto your tunic to denote active service overseas.

ROBERTS How we've managed to sleep at night without chevrons all this time is one of the astounding features of the war!

Nervous laughter.

BARNES If only I'd got me bloomin' chevrons, sir, I'd die happy!

The MEN *laugh again.*

PEARSON Zero minus one.

ROBERTS What's that you're drinking, Dodd?

DODD Water, sir.

ROBERTS Don't you know that water is not for drinking – it's for putting in the radiators of the staff officers' cars.

More laughter.

PEARSON Don't do anything that's risky – forget the water, try some whisky.

PEARSON *hands* DODD *his hip flask.*

DODD Thank you sir.

PEARSON We all need friends to help us through, Dodd...and there's none better than my old chum Johnnie Walker.

PEARSON has a slug himself.

Artillery fire stops.

ROBERTS Good luck everyone. Forward the Foresters. Give the Fritzes hell.

They ready themselves... **ROBERTS** *blows his whistle and they again go over the top... Offstage we hear the horrors of battle. Gunfire, grenades, screams. As the men go over the top they freeze, then turn to face front of stage, as if looking down into a trench.*

Stop! Men! Stop! Cease fire!

There is silence.

ROBERTS, PEARSON *and the* **MEN** *reappearing through the smoke.*

BARNES I don't understand, sir. What happened?

ROBERTS They were already dead. It's the gas. Their own gas. The wind must have changed.

There is a silence.

PEARSON I thought they were a bit...passive.

ROBERTS You mean they didn't put up much of a fight.

PEARSON That's right – not very sporting is it? Signing off before the show has even started.

ROBERTS Spoils the whole fun of the war...

The two **MEN** *know that this is not funny yet they begin to laugh and laugh hysterically until the others all join in and they end up exhausted and weeping with relief and the exaggerated hilarity of combat. Suddenly, more serious.*

PEARSON But what if...

ROBERTS If what?

PEARSON If we'd been a minute earlier...if...

Scene Eleven

On the screen a map of the battlefields highlights the names "Somme", "St. Quentin", "Rosieres" ,"Avre", "Cambrai", "Selle" as the march progresses. We begin with ROBERTS*'s voice, and one by one the* MEN *join in, turning it into a choir of voices, chanting in unison.*

PEARSON

IF YOU CAN LIVE ON BULLY AND A BISCUIT
AND THANK YOUR STARS THAT YOU'VE A TOT OF RUM,
DODGE WHIZZ-BANGS WITH A GRIN AND AS YOU RISK IT
TALK GLIBLY OF THE PRETTY WAY THEY HUM...

PEARSON AND ROBERTS

IF YOU CAN CRAWL THROUGH WIRE AND CRUMP-HOLES REEKING
WITH FEET OF LIQUID MUD, AND KEEP YOUR HEAD
TURNED ALWAYS TO THE PLACE WHICH YOU ARE SEEKING
THROUGH DREAD OF CRYING YOU WILL LAUGH INSTEAD...

ROBERTS, PEARSON, TYLER AND BARNES

IF YOU CAN CLAMBER UP WITH PICK AND SHOVEL
AND TURN YOUR FILTHY CRUMP-HOLE TO A TRENCH
WHEN ALL INSIDE YOU MAKES YOU ITCH TO GROVEL
AND ALL YOU'VE HAD TO FEED ON IS A STENCH

ROBERTS, PEARSON, TYLER, BARNES AND DODD

IF YOU CAN HANG ON JUST BECAUSE YOU ARE THINKING
YOU HAVEN'T GOT ONE CHANCE IN TEN TO LIVE
SO YOU WILL SEE IT THROUGH, NO USE IN BLINKING
AND YOU'RE NOT GOING TO TAKE MORE THAN YOU GIVE

ALL THE MEN, IN UNISON

IF YOU CAN GRIN AT LAST WHEN HANDING OVER
AND FINISH WELL WHAT YOU HAD WELL BEGUN
AND THINK A MUDDY DITCH A BED OF CLOVER
YOU'LL BE A SOLDIER ONE DAY THEN MY SON.

ROBERTS Stand easy. Sergeant, we'll stop here for the night.

The troop disperses, and sets up a makeshift camp – perhaps a tent, table, lantern, bedding roll etcetera.

DODD *approaches* **ROBERTS** *and* **PEARSON** – *he's now a corporal.*

Corporal Dodd?

DODD Sir. We've heard a rumour that the Germans have surrendered.

PEARSON Well if that is the case, corporal someone really ought to tell their artillery.

ROBERTS And if Fritz really **is** waving the white flag then perhaps he could have the decency to stop firing at **us**.

DODD So you don't think it's true sir?

ROBERTS All I am prepared to say is that the tide has apparently turned and perhaps at last we can all look forward to better times.

PEARSON Better Times. That's a good idea for a title.

TYLER *enters.*

TYLER Sir! The advance party has had a major breakthrough.

ROBERTS Really?

TYLER We have located another printing press!

ROBERTS You're a marvel, sergeant!

TYLER The Hun's done his best to prevent any future efforts at journalism by shifting the walls around, melting half the type and filling the office with gas, but it's a finer machine than the last one.

PEARSON Excellent. It means we can carry out our threat of bringing out the paper until the Hun is down and out!

ROBERTS Re-employ Mr Belary Helloc with immediate effect, at his previous enormous salary.

ROBERTS *in makeshift quarters begins working on copy for the* Better Times *newspaper. We see the front page of* Better Times *on screen. The date is 1918. The distant bombardment is still going on.*

Where exactly are we, Jack?

PEARSON *checks maps.*

PEARSON Avesnes.

(He thinks) There was a young man of Avesnes. Took a stroll down a long shady lanes...

ROBERTS He trod on a dud.

PEARSON Half hidden in mud.

ROBERTS He never will do it... Agains...

PEARSON Well up to our usual terrible standard.

ROBERTS Absolutely, and as luck would have it, I've also received a letter to the editor.

PEARSON Is it genuine?

ROBERTS Absolutely. I've just genuinely made it up.

He reads out the letter he has been scribbling.

Dear Sir,

I hear that when it is all over the people who joined up early are going to be demobilised first. This is very unfair since they were obviously much more eager to be in the army than those of us who joined up, reluctantly, later. So surely we should go home sooner?

Yours lance corporal A. Slacker.

PEARSON Very convincing argument...

A big bang shakes the building.

ROBERTS Are you sure about this title, *Better Times*?

PEARSON Apparently all it needs is one last effort and we should bust the Hun completely.

ROBERTS You seem to be suffering from optimism.

PEARSON Talking of which, Tyler reckons we could do a weekly issue.

ROBERTS Why weekly? Why not a daily?

PEARSON **You** seem to be suffering from optimism.

ROBERTS *(laughs)* Guilty. But we are selling like hot cakes.

PEARSON Is that good? I can't even remember what a hot cake tastes like.

ROBERTS We're even selling out on the home front.

PEARSON We would need a lot more copy.

ROBERTS Surely there are enough jokers and more than enough poets out there to fill the space…

> *Their excitement is interrupted by the arrival of* **SERGEANT TYLER** *with a message.*

TYLER Signal for you, sir.

> **ROBERTS** *reads the signal. It reads "Urgent Urgent Urgent Secret Secret Secret".*

ROBERTS *(in shock)* My God!

PEARSON What is it?

ROBERTS It's all over.

TYLER What, sir? Just like that?

ROBERTS *(reads)* Official radio from Paris 6.01 am November 11th 1918 Marshal Foch to the Commander in Chief. Hostilities will be stopped on the entire front beginning at 11 o'clock.

PEARSON So fini la guerre.

ROBERTS Looks like it.

PEARSON Napoo Boche.

ROBERTS So it would seem. It's an armistice.

TYLER No big show then? No final push to Berlin?

> *Pause as the reality sinks in.*

> Shall I tell the men, sir?

ROBERTS Thank you, sergeant. And tell them to keep their bloody heads down until 11 o'clock.

TYLER *salutes and exits, and conveys information to* **BARNES, DODD** *and rest of the* **MEN**.

So Jack, our swords are going to be turned into plough shares. It's the order of the bowler of the hat for us. We're going home.

PEARSON Shouldn't we be celebrating?

ROBERTS I suppose we should.

ROBERTS *holds out his hand to* **PEARSON** *and they shake hands. They hold the position, as if frozen.*

MITFORD *(voiceover)* There was a little Hun, and at war he tried his hand.

And while the Hun was winning, war was fine you understand,

But when the others hit him back he shouted in alarm.

"A little drop of peace wouldn't do me any harm".

Scene Twelve

GENERAL MITFORD *is reading* Better Times *at his desk. Behind him is a large map on the wall of the British army's advances, crossing the Hindenberg Line.* HOWFIELD *enters, handing* MITFORD *some paperwork.*

HOWFIELD So how have your cynical scribbler friends coped with our resounding victory?

MITFORD More of a resounding armistice. Though it's true, the absence of war has injected a note of melancholy into their latest edition.

HOWFIELD After years of sniping at their superiors perhaps they have run out of ammunition?

MITFORD I think that peace brings with it a moment for sober reflection on what's been won and lost – and what the future holds. Of course they say they're heartily glad the whole ghastly affair is over, and they congratulate the few original members of the division who made it through to the end – but the editors also remember those who are not with us, but lie in France or Belgium.

He reads.

"Our reverence and love be with them and they will never be forgotten."

HOWFIELD *(mollified)* Indeed. That's as may be. But now that we've actually **won** the war I hope they will treat the Staff with a little more respect.

MITFORD Their account of the moment of victory does pay tribute to the fighting qualities of the General Staff.

HOWFIELD I'm very pleased to hear it.

MITFORD *(reading)* "Eleven hundred hours on the 11th of November was zero hour, and the red hats attacked in mass".

HOWFIELD What?!

MITFORD "The barrage of paper fell right on our trenches, and mixed with the high explosive was **gas** in enormous quantities".

HOWFIELD *(angry)* The cessation of hostilities inevitably entails a substantial element of bureaucracy! Someone has to balance the books. Someone has to account for the war.

MITFORD I think that will be up to history.

HOWFIELD I will not have it! We are NOT the enemy!

MITFORD No, no, of course not. They do appreciate that. Which is why they are recommending the Staff be awarded more medals.

HOWFIELD About time.

MITFORD *(reads)* They want special recognition for all those martyrs who had to endure wearying years of soft jobs at the base and missed out on all the fun of the front line.

HOWFIELD Well let's see how funny they find life on civvy street!

Music hall music strikes up.

Scene Thirteen

Music hall.

We are back in ROBERTS's *fantasy world of the music hall, with the* MASTER OF CEREMONIES.

MC And welcome back to the European Theatre for our grand finale featuring Professor Foch and his performing dove!

Audience cheers.

We see on the screen archive still of Field Marshall Foch leading negotiations for the armistice.

Sadly Kaiser Bill Hohenzollern will not be appearing as he has an alternative engagement singing "My old Dutch" in Holland.

We see archive still of the Kaiser escaping to Holland.

Audience boos.

And also not on the bill are – the famous crumps!

Audience cheers.

We see rows of decommissioned artillery guns. There are no sound effects of explosions just silence.

And the little pipsqueaks!

Audience cheers again.

We see another silent battery.

And duddy whizz-bang!

We see still of silent artillery.

Yes, the show mustn't go on! You've seen the Horrors of War. Now prepare for the Horrors of Peace!

Audience laughs.

You were an army of occupation. And now you are going to be an army of no occupation.

Audience boos.

So without further ado let us have one last encore from Tommy Atkins and Co with a delightfully delicious ditty – costumes kindly provided by Messrs D Mob and Co – the celebrated tailors of Cheap Street.

Piano strikes up.

On stage we see PEARSON *and all the* MEN *stripping off their army uniforms and putting on ill-fitting demob suits in choreographed routine.*

ALL

SO SCRAP THE MORTAR MINE AND SHELL,
THE JOBS COMPLETELY DONE AND WELL,
WE'RE DONE WITH MUD AND RATS AND STENCH,
FAREWELL TO ROTTING IN A TRENCH.

MC That will do lads, we don't want to end the show on a low note.

The MEN *resume singing.*

ALL

NO MORE WE'LL HEAR THE SOUNDS OF WAR,
THE MINNIES DIN,THE BIG GUNS ROAR,
THE LONG LAST YEARS HAVE BEEN WELL WORTH,
IF ONCE AGAIN WE'VE PEACE ON EARTH.

MC That's more like it. Now come on everybody, let's see that demobilisation smile.

Everyone puts on cheesy grin.

ALL

FAREWELL TO YOU, TO DEAR OLD WIPERS,
FOR BETTER TIMES HAVE COME TO PASS,
AND IF YOU ASK US BACK TO FLANDERS,
WE'LL ALL SAY SHOVE IT UP YOUR...

MC *(interrupting, banging his* MC'*s hammer)* A little decorum, gentlemen, please! You are **not** in the army now!

Blackout.

Scene Fourteen

Newspaper office.

We are back in the oak-panelled newspaper editor's office. The DEPUTY EDITOR *has been perusing* The Wipers Times. *He hands it back to him.*

DEPUTY EDITOR All very amusing – but I am not sure that it is **journalism**. Nowadays ours is a very modern, high-pressure business.

ROBERTS Have you ever sat in a trench in the middle of a battle and corrected page proofs? You should try it.

DEPUTY EDITOR I am sure – but that was quite a long time ago. Your CV is a bit sketchy on your more recent career.

ROBERTS I went back to prospecting. Spent some time in Africa looking for gold, had some ups...and some downs, came home and thought I would have a last shot at something people were kind enough to say I was good at. I thought if old Teach Bomas...sorry Beach Thomas can get a job then surely I was in with a chance.

The DEPUTY EDITOR *does not laugh.*

DEPUTY EDITOR He's **Sir** William Beach Thomas and he's one of our most distinguished correspondents.

ROBERTS Of course. I'm sorry. Only he was a bit of a joke in the war.

DEPUTY EDITOR Yes...we're not really interested in "jokes". Modern writers tell the **truth** about the war.

ROBERTS *(getting very annoyed)* Then perhaps I should write you a harrowing article about how all was **not** quiet on the western front. How with shells raining down upon us and the chilly November air being rent with fury, the sub-editor and I drank a case of whisky, shot the padre for cowardice, and said "Goodbye To All That"?

DEPUTY EDITOR That's more like it!

ROBERTS *(holding up* The Wipers Times, *now very angry)* **No –
this** was **my** truth.

ROBERTS *starts to get up.*

I'm sorry for wasting your time.

DEPUTY EDITOR No, don't be so hasty. There's no need to go
over the... (top). Here's the thing: I like you, Mr Roberts – I
really do – and it's clear you're clever with words, so I think
I might have something for you here at the Daily News.

ROBERTS *sits down interestedly.*

How about you start work on the...crossword?

ROBERTS *is utterly deflated.*

ROBERTS You want me to compile the crossword?

DEPUTY EDITOR No. **Help** compile the crossword. See how it
goes. Better not rush things.

ROBERTS It's not exactly the front line of the circulation war.

DEPUTY EDITOR A chap in your position can't expect too much.
What do you think?

ROBERTS I think...

ROBERTS *looks wistfully above him and a large cartoon
bomb on a wire descends slowly towards the head of
the* **DEPUTY EDITOR.** *We hear the whistle sound of a
falling bomb. Suddenly there is a loud bang as the bomb
explodes and the lights go out. This is in* **ROBERTS's**
*imagination. When the lights come back on again the
bomb has gone and the* **DEPUTY EDITOR** *is still sitting
at his desk.*

DEPUTY EDITOR I said what do you think?

ROBERTS *smiles, collects his papers and coat, gets up
from his chair and strides out of the office through the
auditorium. The* **DEPUTY EDITOR** *calls out after him.*

You haven't given me an answer Mr Roberts! Mr Roberts –
do you want this job or not? Mr Roberts...

But **ROBERTS** *has gone. There is a pause and then* **PEARSON** *appears in a spotlight at the back of the stage, and addresses the audience.*

PEARSON Probably not Fleet Street's finest hour. Captain Fred Roberts MC was never published again. Instead he resumed his mining career and spent his last years living in Canada.

On the screen we see a breathtaking view of the Rockies. **ROBERTS** *joins* **PEARSON** *in the spotlight.*

ROBERTS I tried to join up again in 1940 when friend Fritz demanded a replay but the brass hats said I was too old. Damned cheek – I was only fifty five!

PEARSON *laughs.*

Lieutenant Jack Pearson DSO MC also left England and moved to Argentina where he worked as a railway engineer.

On the screen we see breathtaking view of the Sierra de Cordoba. **PEARSON** *appears in another spotlight next to* **ROBERTS** *wearing a linen suit and panama hat.*

PEARSON Married a local girl and took over her parents' hotel. So ended up as mein host.

ROBERTS Fitting career.

PEARSON But I never forgot the friends I made back then and the friend that helped me get through the war was without doubt...

ROBERTS *waits for warm tribute to their friendship.*

...Johnny Walker

ROBERTS *laughs.*

Snifter?

He raises a glass to **ROBERTS**.

ROBERTS Neither of us received an entry in Who's Who or an obituary in the London Times.

The light fades on the two men but on the screen we see the front page of The Wipers Times, *starting as a dot and getting bigger and bigger until it fills the whole screen.*

But our legacy was, and is, *The Wipers Times.*

Blackout.

After the 2nd curtain call TYLER *calls the cast to attention and conducts them in a final rendition of The Whisky Song.*

CAST

THERE ARE VARIOUS TYPES OF COURAGE
THERE ARE MANY KINDS OF FEAR
THERE ARE MANY BRANDS OF WHISKY
THERE ARE MANY MAKES OF BEER
THERE IS ALSO RUM WHICH SOMETIMES
IN OUR NEED CAN HELP US MUCH
BUT TIS WHISKY WHISKY WHISKY HANDS
THE COURAGE WHICH IS DUTCH...

HERE ARE VARIOUS TYPES OF VALOUR
THERE ARE MANY KINDS OF FUNK
THERE ARE MANY MAKES OF BRANDY
MANY WINES WHICH MUST BE DRUNK
THERE IS ALSO GIN WHICH SOMETIMES
IN OUR NEED CAN HELP US MUCH
BUT TIS WHISKY WHISKY WHISKY HANDS
THE COURAGE WHICH IS DUTCH...

Ends

PROPERTY LIST

Furniture
Large writing desk
Small bureau writing desk
Small wooden table
Printer
Wheelchair
Chairs
Camera on tripod
Two beer barrels
Ammunition boxes
Tables for the Ritz
Portable desk
Props
Oil lamp
Typewriter
Paper tray
Telephone
Briefcase
Rifles and bayonets
Tarpaulin x 2
Sledgehammer
Lumps of shrapnel, masonry
Gramophone – in the den, practical, needs to wind up and turn
Whisky bottles – throughout Johnnie Walker label
Tin cups
Printing tray
Printing blocks
Glass tumblers – cut glass, in HQ
Stethoscope
Wire cutters
Watering can – sprinkler
Swanee whistle
Blocks of type for "Tip-me-up" duck board
More printers blocks
Shovels
Field telephone
Printer parts incl. a mangled wheel
New, small printer
Rifles x2 Trench and Foote
Blackboard
Glass of water
Champagne glasses
Champagne bottle
Fairy lights or red paper shades – to set the scene at Madame
Fifi's. Strung between balconies.
Knapsack – Four bags currently needed
Champagne bottle and glass
Rum jug for rum ration

Bed roll
Two linen table cloths
Wine glasses
Wine decanter
Debris dinners at the Ritz – leftovers on Roberts's table and on another table as drunken diners leave
Bandage – Pearson's hand
Sack of mail – submissions to the paper.
Gas masks
Gas bells – rung on stage
Flagon of beer
Decanter and glasses – posh ones. Mitford pours back in
Hip flask
Hurricane lamp
Gavel
Binoculars
Paper props
Somme Times
Copy of the Daily Mail
Letters from home – from Kate to Roberts, and from Pearson's wife
New Church Times – permission to take photos for Michelin guides
Land and Water magazine   – inside case, incl copy of WT, CV
Map of Ypres – the finest accommodation in Ypres
Banknotes (French?) – hand painted
Permit papers – Mitford is reading these
Pockmarked road sign for Ypres – many, throughout, will get damaged through use and need multiples
Boxes of paper
Papers
Long casualty lists
Page proofs
Paper and pens and pencils
Notebooks, pencils
Signal – end of war
Signs – on a wire / arm
Sign "Hotel des Ramparts"
Picadilly Circus sign – Pearson's personal
Sign "Hotel des Ramparts Special Christmas Menu"
Attempt at Christmas tree with star
Printer issue of WT volume 1
Cartoon bomb
Home made pub sign
Forester's Arms signboard
Consumables
Cigarettes
Wine
Champagne bottle, corked
Whisky

www.ingramcontent.com/pod-product-compliance
Lightning Source LLC
Chambersburg PA
CBHW071353090426
42738CB00012B/3099